No greater love

No greater love

The Martyrs of the Middlesbrough Diocese

Roland Connelly

McCRIMMONS
Great Wakering Essex

First published in 1987 by McCrimmon Publishing Co Ltd
Great Wakering, Essex, England

ISBN 0 85597 391 9

Cover design by Nick Snode
Typeset by Permanent Typesetting & Printing Co. Ltd., Hong Kong

Acknowledgements

The writer is grateful to all who helped in the preparation of this work, and expresses his thanks particularly to:

Trudie Thompson for the map work,
Leo Cook for the photography
and Bernard Connelly

Contents

Illustrations

Maps

Foreword

Eighty-five English and Welsh martyrs are currently being considered for beatification. From these Father Roland Connelly, SM, has selected twenty-nine whom he considers to have some ties with the present Diocese of Middlesbrough, but we of the diocese are quite prepared to share them. All the English and Welsh Martyrs are very near to us. Their names are our names. Their cause is our cause. Their integrity, their refusal to betray conscience—this is admired by friend and foe alike. Every single martyr would today be protected under the Helsinki Agreement. They would be highlighted as prisoners of conscience. Amnesty International would rise to defend them.

But there is more to their story. They died for their faith. They died to perpetuate the Mass and remain one with the See of Peter. On the first evening of the visit of Pope John Paul to Britain a crowd gathered outside Westminster Cathedral. They had waited long for this moment. And they began to chant: "We want Peter". Yes, those were the words. The martyrs had made their point.

When, for the first time in history, a Pope set foot in Yorkshire, he landed near the spot where Constantine was first acclaimed as Emperor and on the very spot where martyrs gave their lives to remain one with Peter. On the Knavesmire, York, there are now two stone memorials, one marking the spot where the martyrs died, the other marking the spot where a Pope was welcomed by people of many faiths and none. The Memorial stone is a gift from the Dean and Chapter of York Minster. The memorial was erected by the citizens of York. Would our martyrs be at ease in the Church today? They were no strangers to change. While their country was being robbed of the faith their whole life-style had to change and the later martyrs even introduced a new rite of celebrating Mass—the Tridentine Rite. Of one thing we may be sure—they would test the integrity of any change by turning to 'Peter'. For them the Vatican Council of the twentieth century would have the same authority as the Council of Trent in the sixteenth century. Their martyrdom was and is a stand for a Church which can guide us through authentic development. It is our martyrs who make us feel relaxed in change because they have held us close to the one who sets his seal on change.

The threats to our faith in the twentieth century are a far cry from those of the sixteenth and seventeenth centuries. But the threats are still real. The very freedom to worship and the religious tolerance in our country leave us vulnerable to subtle temptations. The true pilgrim way to God is never smooth and we are foolish if we think it so. There is no easy option for those who follow Christ and the martyrs are living again in this book so that we may walk their way. It is for this purpose that Father Connelly was asked to chronicle the lives and deaths of our fellow Catholics. These pages are not remote records. They are sermons for today—a stirring of twentieth century Catholics so that, having our faith saved by sacrifice, we may not let it slip away because of our own mediocrity.

Father Connelly has worked long and skilfully to help us know our martyrs. He has researched honestly to find the truth whether it be in records or oral traditions or deductions from both. He has blended scholarship with easy reading. He has shared his life long enthusiasm for the martyrs and we are deep in his debt. Because of his work we have a lively knowledge of our martyrs. May that knowledge be matched by our sharpened spirituality so that the faith of our fathers may be living still.

AUGUSTINE HARRIS
Bishop of Middlesbrough.

28 August, 1986
The Feast of St. Augustine of Hippo

Introduction: The Martyrs

On 21 September, 1978, Cardinal Basil Hume, Archbishop of Westminster signed the final documents concerning 'The Fact, Cause and Constancy' of another eighty-five English Martyrs, and even as he put his signature to the paper, the former Abbot of Ampleforth must have smiled a little smile that so many of these Martyrs were from the homeland of his own monastery in the Diocese of Middlesbrough.

Like all the other English Martyrs of the sixteenth and seventeenth centuries, these Martyrs have been under investigation for a long time. It was in 1643, that the Holy See, at the request of the English Benedictines in exile first set up the Official Process to collect and examine the evidence for martyrdom claimed for so many priests and lay-people, but the work was impeded by the difficult state of affairs in England itself, where persecution still raged. It was not until the more relaxed days of the nineteenth century and especially after the Restoration of the Hierarchy in 1850 that progress could be made.

In 1874, Archbishop (later Cardinal) Henry Edward Manning inaugurated a Commission at Westminster to speed up the work of investigation, and such were the enthusiasms of the times that active consideration was given at once to three hundred and sixty-one possible Martyrs. By 1895, sixty-three of these had been accepted by the Roman Authorities and were accorded the title of 'Blessed'.

The momentum of the Westminster Commission, unfortunately, could not be maintained, and for the next thirty years the undoubted interest and devotion of many Catholics could not be reflected in the results of the work of the Commission. It was not until 1923, when Cardinal Francis Bourne called for a new effort, that further progress was made. Within six years, two hundred and thirty-four Martyrs were cleared for formal beatification, although in fact only one hundred and thirty-six were beatified in 1929. The other ninety-eight, including all the martyrs in this present study, were said to need further examination 'in order that their martyrdom might be more clearly manifested'.

And so the members of the Commission returned to work on these 'delayed' martyrs, only to find themselves diverted from their general task by the great upsurge of popular devotion in the 1930's for two particular Martyrs, Blessed Thomas More and Blessed John Fisher. A massive petition was organised from all the Catholics of England and Wales, and in response Pope Pius XI asked for the immediate presentation of their Cause. As a result, both were canonised as Saints on 19 May, 1935, and only then did it seem that consideration could be given once more to the Causes of the 'delayed' Martyrs.

Sadly, there followed another period of difficulty. Conditions for study were not easy. The Second World War intervened and caused inevitable disruption, and on the conclusion of the War there were more distractions within the Church. Once more the Commission was diverted from its main task. In 1960, the Bishops of England and Wales began to press for the canonisation of a representative group of Martyrs, already declared Blessed, and only when these Forty Martyrs became Saints in 1970 could proper attention be given to the 'delayed' Martyrs of 1929.

Now at last the times seemed propitious. There was a new enthusiasm in the air. The religious excitement associated with the canonisation of the Forty Martyrs produced an increase in devotion to all the martyrs, and all this just at the time when modern historical scholars were discovering a new interest in recusant history, and ecumenists were sweeping away the old misunderstanding that Catholic devotion to their Martyrs was an obstacle on the way to Church Unity.

Encouraged by the generous statement of the British Council of Churches (17 December, 1969) which recognised the importance to the Catholic Church of the veneration of her Martyrs and declared with satisfaction that the different Christian denominations 'acknowledge the martyr tradition as one in which all have shared, and from which all may draw strength even across denominational boundaries', the members of the Commission applied themselves to their work with a new determination.

With the passage of years it had become no easier task. Modern standards of historical scholarship are high and the search for 16th century certainty depends so much on the documents available. It was soon realised that the evidence in support of some Martyrs was insufficient to meet the demands of a critical world, and accordingly thirty-one were dropped from the proceedings.

The remaining eighty-five became the subjects of a most intense and scholarly historical examination as the attempt was made in each case to prove that the individual had willingly given up his life for his Faith and that his contemporaries recognised his death as a true martyrdom. But to find written evidence to attest these facts was a time-consuming exercise often doomed to failure.

The sixteenth century is not a good time for records. The passage of the years has taken its toll and many Court reports and Government documents have been lost. Only occasionally was it possible to find official papers referring to the arrest, trial and execution of the Martyrs.

Nor was it any easier to find written information from the Catholics of the time. Living in fear of an oppressive law, they were slow to commit to paper anything which might incriminate themselves or their friends. They used codes and assumed names and wrote in riddles. Even as late as the eighteenth century, priests would refer to the Pope as Mr Peters of Hilton, and report the spiritual state of their flock as if they were grocers engaged in stock-taking.

In the early days of the Persecution, communication among Catholics depended almost entirely on the spoken word. Facts were passed by word of mouth and only when one of the parties went overseas to Douai or some other English place of refuge would the attempt be made to write down as much information as could be recollected.

In such circumstances, documentary evidence for the Martyrs is not over-abundant, and what is available is often fragmentary and sometimes confusing. Nevertheless, there is sufficient to compile factual accounts of the lives and deaths of those Martyrs under consideration, and if at times details seem sparse and gaps appear in the narrative, the hope still remains that as time goes on more and more of the better-hidden documents will appear.

Of particular value in all this historical research are the existing Catalogues of Martyrs, compiled by individuals but also reflecting the widespread belief of their contemporaries. The first of these Catalogues was printed in 1585 and is attributed to Father Nicholas Sanders and Father Edward Rishton. Within the next one hundred years more than twenty such lists were published, and of these thirteen are dated prior to 1620. Bishop Richard Smith's Chalcedon Catalogue of 1628 has an authority all its own.

All these scattered records have proved their value, but tribute must be paid to those who collected and preserved these papers as well as to those who wrote them. Cardinal William Allen began the process of collecting documents at Douai from 1582 onwards. His work was continued by the indefatigable Father Christopher Grene SJ (1629–1697), who, prevented by ill-health from working on the English Mission, spent his years collecting and transcribing appropriate documents, and in the words of Father John Morris SJ 'did more than any other man to save the records of their suffering from perishing and to transmit to us materials for the history of the time of persecution in England'.

Another major contribution was made at a later date by Bishop Richard Challoner (1691–1781), who collected the available materials and then used them to write his remarkable book, *Memoirs of Missionary Priests*, which is still an essential source book for any study of the English Martyrs. His writing is always close to his documents and his work has an added importance because many of the sources he used have subsequently been lost.

From such records and writings, the case for the official recognition of the Martyrs has been built up, and the facts of death and the reasons for execution established, but each case depends also on the reactions of the Catholics of the time and the underlying, vital question to be answered is always, 'Did the people of his time accept that this person was truly a Martyr for his Faith?'

Sometimes this question can be answered very easily from a

living tradition. The search for relics at the time of death and subsequent devotion to such relics are powerful signs of a martyr's cult. Claims that miracles have been worked through the Martyr's intercession and that prayers have been answered all testify to the same belief. In a certain sense, saints are made by popular acclamation; official canonisation merely puts the seal of Church approval on what the people have already decided, but the final decision rests with the Holy See and depends upon the strength of the case presented.

It will be a long, long time before all the English Martyrs of the sixteenth and seventeenth centuries receive formal recognition by the Church. The present work on the presentation of Causes concentrates on seeking the Beatification and Canonisation of only the eighty-five 'Venerable Servants of God, put to death in England and Wales and Scotland in defence of the Catholic Faith (1584–1679).' The Catholics of England look forward to honouring these fellow-countrymen of theirs as Saints, while the people of the Diocese of Middlesbrough in particular rejoice that no fewer than twenty-nine of these Venerable Servants of God are connected with their Diocese by their birth, their death or their work, and it is these Martyrs who are commemorated in the following pages.

The Diocese of Middlesbrough

The geographical expression of the Middlesbrough Diocese extends across Yorkshire from the waters of the Ure and Ouse in the west to the beaches and cliffs of the east coast; and from the Tees in the north to the Humber in the south.

The people of the Diocese live in the old North and East Ridings with the addition of the ancient city of York. The Catholics of Richmondshire and Holderness, of Cleveland and Howdenshire are joined to the Catholics of the Moors and the Wolds to form a local Church which thanks God for the past and prays with faith for the present and the future.

The Diocese itself is only a little over one hundred years old and most of its people endure the sprawling industrial conurbations of Teesside and Humberside, but beyond these areas are older parishes in the wide-open Yorkshire countryside, where constant reminders of a rich Catholic heritage link the Church of today with the Faith of our Fathers. For the Catholics of this region are an ancient people and the roots of their faith are buried deep in the soils of time.

More than a thousand years ago, the fair-haired young men who caught the eye of Pope St Gregory the Great in the Roman market place were recognised as natives of Deira, that formidable Northumbrian kingdom which stretched from Tees to Humber. It was for the conversion of these people that St Paulinus was sent by papal mandate to preach the Gospel to King Edwin, and in the year 627 both Ouse and Swale were used to baptise the thousands of new Christians.

The Celtic saints came down from the north, from Iona and Lindisfarne and from across the Irish Sea. They brought the true

Faith but a different observance, and at Whitby in 664, Celt and Roman came together in one historic council to establish the unity of the Local Church, which grew and prospered to embrace all men.

The glorious minsters of York and Beverley today bear witness to an ancient faith and a universal belief, and those with eyes to see contemplate with proud sorrow the persisting testimony of the monastic remains of Rievaulx and Bylands, Easby and Jervaulx, Lastingham and Meaux.

But buildings are only signs of Faith; the reality lies in the hearts and minds of men, and the people of the Diocese of Middlesbrough today are blessed and strengthened by so many acknowledged saints, who belong to them in a special way because they once lived in this land and called it 'home'.

St Aelred of Rievaulx, St William of York, St John of Bridlington, St Hilda of Whitby, St John of Beverley, all belong in this way, as a constant reminder to the little people of today that, with God's help, holiness is within their reach.

The local church of Deira became the splendid medieval Church of York, and all seemed well for many years until the black shadow of the Tudors appeared in the south. The people of Yorkshire stood firm when the storm burst in the sixteenth century. One of the first to profess his faith in defiance of the King's will was St John Fisher of Beverley. He paid the price gladly on Tower Hill in London on 22 June, 1535.

The next year, the common people of Howdenshire and Richmondshire and Cleveland flocked to the banner of the Five Wounds of Christ bravely raised by Robert Aske of Aughton in the East Riding; but it was all in vain, armed rebellion could not succeed, and the Pilgrimage of Grace was a glorious failure.

Robert Aske was hanged in chains from the very top of Clifford's Tower and for many days the citizens of York were forced to watch his lingering death. Executions took place both far and near. Bridlington lost its Prior, William Wood; Jervaulx its Abbot, Adam Sedburgh. In the North Riding, Sir John Bulmer of Wilton Castle gave his life; so did Sir Robert Constable of Flamborough in the East Riding. And many more, unknown, uncounted, died as martyrs for the faith they loved. Official recognition by the Church can never be theirs, but they hold an honoured place in the memories of all who share their Faith.

And true martyrs there were in plenty: St Margaret Clitherow of York, St Luke Kirby SJ, reputedly from Bedale, and St Henry Walpole SJ, who landed at Flamborough, was captured at Kilham and died in York.

Among the one hundred and fifty-seven English Martyrs, whose Causes have progressed so far at Rome that they are officially styled 'Blessed', no fewer than twenty-nine are connected to the Middlesbrough Diocese by reason of their birth, their work or their death.

But of course the full list of those who died for the Faith can never be completed. Many died in obscurity and not even their names are known today. Others simply disappeared into the infamous prisons of York and the Blockhouses of Hull to die a lingering death from hunger, cold and disease. Nor should the heroic role be overlooked of those confessors who were prepared to offer their lives but who were denied the martyr's crown. Such people spent long years in prison, paid heavy fines, were pursued by a relentless Law and often lived as strangers in their own land.

The local priests, like all the priests of their time, were forced to lead a hidden life as hunted criminals. In a sense, the martyrs were those who failed; the successful priest was the one who evaded his searchers, and the measure of his success was that he never left any traces of his presence. Very little is known about these courageous confessors, but their stature and importance is undoubted. They were men like Father John Mush in York and Father Richard Holtby SJ, the organisers of the Mission for the North-East, who shared the dangers and played a major role in preserving the Faith for which the martyrs died.

Priests and lay people worked together for self-protection, and the people of the Middlesbrough Diocese should never forget the debt they owe to the staunch Catholic families on whom the missionary priests depended for their very lives: the Babthorpes of Babthorpe and Osgodby, the Constables of Everingham and Burton Constable, the Lawsons of Brough Park, the Scropes of Danby, the Fairfaxes of Gilling, the Langdales of Holme on Spalding Moor, the Meynells of Yarm and Kilvington, and so many more, who disregarded their own safety and risked their wealth, their property and their freedom to ensure the constant ministry of the priest.

From this historic background emerged the modern Diocese of Middlesbrough, its inheritance enhanced and its community strengthened by people moving in from other places. Who could ever measure the extraordinary achievements of the Irish priests and people in the past and in the present? The real success is known to God alone, but the signs of success are visible to all. And there are other, smaller groups who have played a not insignificant part in this growth of a people: the Polish and Italian communities; the almost-forgotten French émigré priests of the early nineteenth century and the Belgian priests of this century; and all the more recent arrivals from other parts of England.

This is the Local Church of today. All belong and all have given something of themselves to form the People of God in this area, and all are proud to share their gift of faith as spiritual children of their local ancestors. The arduous labours and heroic devotion of the past bear rich fruit today, and many different people form one community. All united in one Diocese, they have the encouragement and inspiration of the example of holy predecessors as the work of preaching the Gospel to all who live twixt Tees and Humber is continued and developed. And all know full well that for that noble work, they have the strength of God from the constant intercession of so many local saints in heaven, and so many martyrs who gave their lives that their children might have eternal life.

DIOCESE OF MIDDLESBROUGH : EAST RIDING

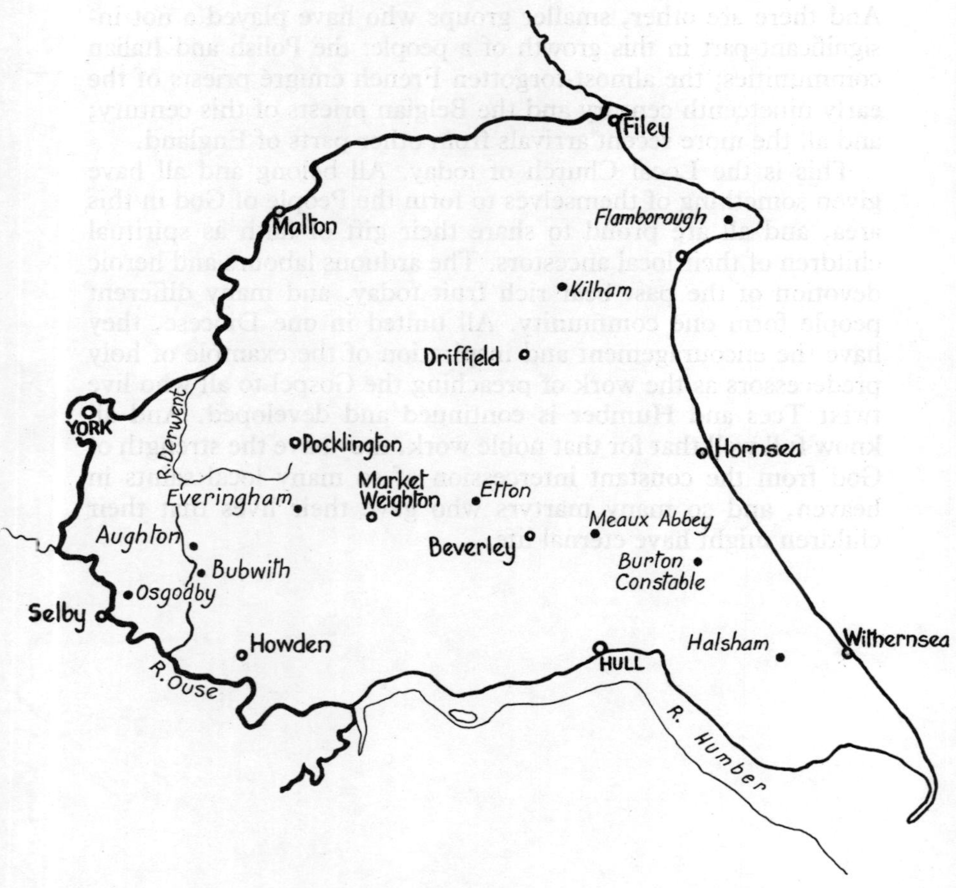

Sketch Map of HOWDENSHIRE AREA

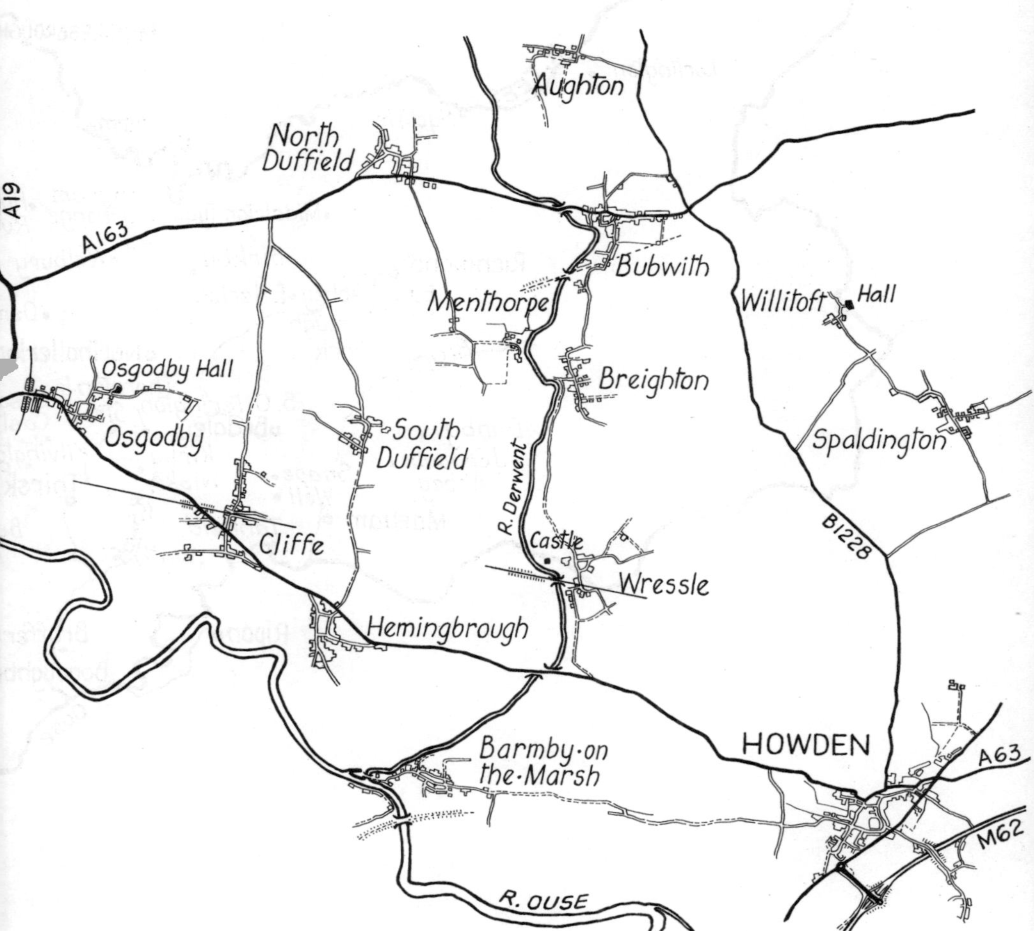

DIOCESE OF MIDDLESBROUGH

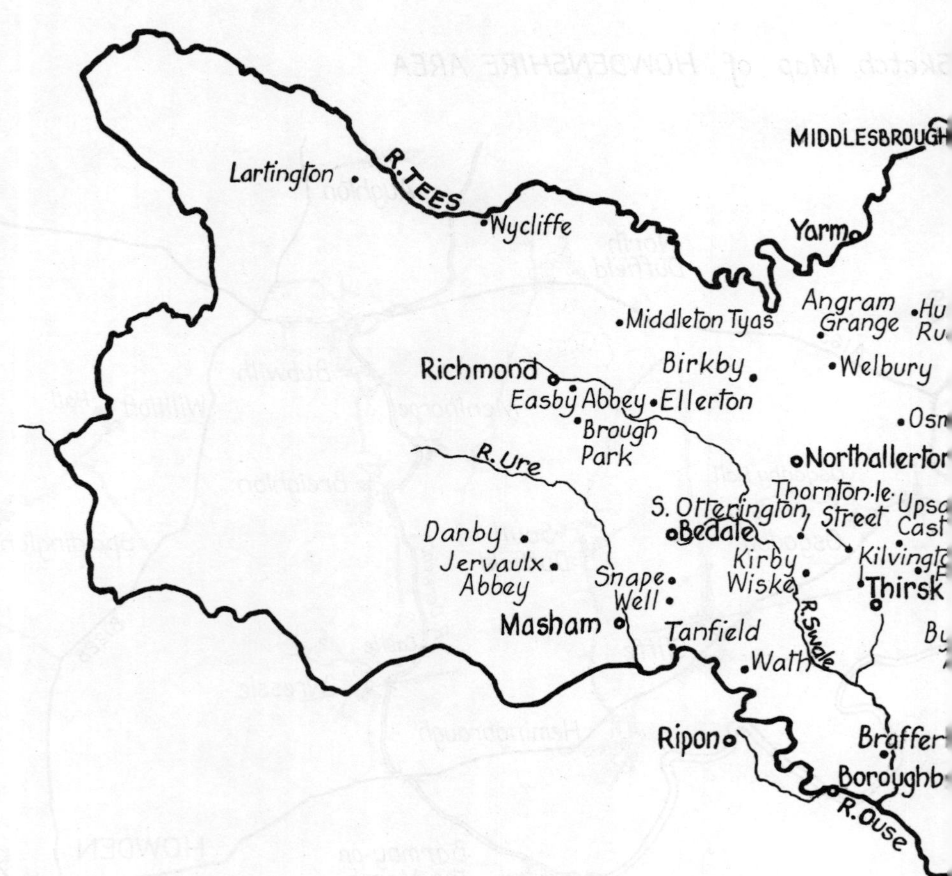

NORTH RIDING

Hugh Taylor

The most infamous of all the Penal Laws passed by Queen Elizabeth against her Catholic subjects was the Act of 1585, which was styled, 'An Act against Jesuits, seminary priests and such other like disobedient persons'. By this Act, it became high treason for any Englishman ordained abroad as a Catholic priest after 24 June, 1559, to come into or remain in England.

This Act was the culmination of all the Elizabethan penal legislation, which had begun in 1559, the very first year of her reign. Catholics had suffered under these severe laws and the death penalty was not uncommon, but under this new Act any priest ordained overseas by the Pope's authority was to be guilty of high treason by merely setting foot in his own country. No further proof of sedition was required; the Act presumed to make the priest a traitor; and the punishment for high treason was death in its most barbaric form: the victim being hanged, drawn and quartered.

Among the priests in England when this new Act came into force on 9 May, 1585 was Father Hugh Taylor. He would be at this time somewhere in Yorkshire or Durham, and was just beginning his apostolate, having returned to England from Douai on 27 March, 1585. He must have heard of this new Law but he could not have known that he was to be the first priest to suffer under its provisions.

The fact that Father Hugh Taylor was working in the north-east of England is not conclusive proof that he was a native of this district, although it was common practice for the newly-arrived priest to make for his own home territory where he knew the land and he knew the people. Bishop Richard Smith, who always made a special effort to be accurate, states in the Chalcedon Catalogue (1628) that Hugh Taylor was born in Durham, but whether he means city, county or diocese is not clear.

From his date of ordination it is estimated that his date of birth would be probably about or shortly before 1560.

Nothing more is known of the early life of Hugh Taylor until he presented himself on 7 May, 1582 at the English College, Douai, then in exile at Rheims. With him was his brother Henry, but only Hugh persevered in his studies for the priesthood. Henry left the seminary and later married.

The Douai diary shows that after completing his studies in two years, Father Hugh Taylor was ordained to the priesthood at Soissons on 13 June, 1584. He then remained overseas for nine months before returning to England. On 24 November, he was on trial for his life.

The details of his arrest and trial are given in a contemporary paper, probably written by Father John Mush in the late sixteenth century and preserved in Father Christopher Grene's Collection E. This states, 'At the gaol delivery before Christmas last, anno domini 1585, the 28th year of Elizabeth's reign, they executed one priest as traitor, named Mr Hugh Taylor, taken by the Lord Evers when he searched a Catholic man's house. This martyr was the first that suffered here since the statutes. They alleged no other matter against him but that he was a seminary priest, and for this they put him to a traitor's death'.

The same document makes it very clear that Father Taylor was not captured as has been generally supposed at the house of Mr Marmaduke Bowes, at Angram Grange near Northallerton. The document attributed to Father Mush continues, 'At this time also they murdered a secular gentleman called Mr Bowes for harbouring the same priest long before he was apprehended in another man's house'.

Father Taylor was tried before the Council of the North in York. The President, Henry Hastings, Third Earl of Huntingdon, was not present, but in his place was the Vice-President, William, Second Baron Evers, the very man who had arrested the priest in the first place. With him as Judges were Laurence Mears, Ralph Hurlestone, and Henry Cheeke, all members of the Council of the North.

There are reports from 1614 and 1628 that Hugh Taylor was condemned on three charges: (1) reconciling Her Majesty's subjects to the Apostolic See, (2) denying the Royal Supremacy, (3) being found in England as a priest. But the contemporary statement, quoted above and attributed to Father Mush is quite clear, 'They alleged no other matter against him but that he was a seminary priest. . .' For this, he was condemned to death, and another completely anonymous paper of 1586 in Father Christopher Grene's Collection E describes his final hours: 'Taylor, having been condemned to death in company with a layman on Thursday, was able to celebrate Mass and recite his Office on the Friday. Then he said, "How happy I should be if on this day on which Christ died for me, I might encounter death for Him". Scarcely had he said this, when the officer unexpectedly came to lead him off to execution, and leaving the layman for Saturday, (the customary day for executions) put him immediately to death'.

Father Hugh Taylor was hanged, drawn and quartered at York on 26 November, 1585.

Marmaduke Bowes

Father Hugh Taylor's companion in martyrdom was Mr Marmaduke Bowes, one of the laymen who had befriended him, and their execution in York stirred up the indignation of the Catholic community throughout the county.

News travelled slowly in those days of secrecy but information about the death of Mr Bowes was passed on by word of mouth with such speed, that in a very short time every Catholic in Yorkshire was aware of what had happened, and the fact that Bowes was a layman only served to heighten their interest and concern.

Rumours captured the Catholic imagination. It was said that Marmaduke Bowes had been executed merely for giving a cup of beer at his door to a priest. This story is quoted by Bishop Richard Smith in the Chalcedon Returns of 1620 on the evidence of Mr Leonard Brackenbury, an attorney of the time. The same report had reached Lady Grace Babthorpe, living far away in the East Riding at Osgodby, but she did not associate it with Marmaduke Bowes. Another Yorkshire lawyer, Mr John Ingleby of Lawkland in the West Riding, makes the following statement in the Chalcedon Returns: 'Mr Bowes of Angram Grange, near Appleton in Cleveland; a priest being taken at his house, he comes to York at the Assizes to free the priest by his appearance; whereupon so soon as he was lighted from his horse, without pulling off his boots (as the manner then was after a journey) he goes straight to the castle yard to speak in the priest's behalf. But himself being thereupon also questioned, he was condemned and executed for harbouring the aforesaid priest'. Such detail is of interest and certainly the story of the layman who was condemned for giving a cup of beer to a priest and then executed with his boots on figures prominently in Catholic tradition.

Lady Grace Babthorpe is more exact in the account she gave specifically about Marmaduke Bowes. She wrote these narrations late in life about the year 1620 when she was about to be professed as a nun with the Canonesses of St Augustine at St Monica's Convent, Louvain, but her memory of what had happened thirty-five years before seems very clear. Father Alban Butler inspected her manuscript for Bishop Richard Challoner in the early seventeenth century and complained about her writing and her spelling, but the testimony of a woman who had suffered so much for her faith is invaluable. She wrote, 'There was a gentleman, one Mr Bowes, a married man, who had a wife and children and kept a schoolmaster to teach his children. The schoolmaster accused his master for receiving priests into his house. This fellow was a Catholic and so came to know such men for priests which his master entertained, but the gentleman himself was no Catholic but a good schismatic. Upon his schoolmaster's accusation to the Council at York, this Mr Bowes was sent for to answer this complaint made of him, after which he was suffered to go home, and to appear again at the Assizes, which he did, thinking himself secure, but at his coming again he was presently indicted, condemned and hanged and, as it was reported, in his boots and spurs as he came to the town. He died very willingly and professed his faith with great repentance that he lived in schism'. As befits a cautious old lady, Lady Babthorpe is a little short on names but there is no doubt that Marmaduke Bowes lived at Ingram or Angram Grange, which is situated close to Welbury near Northallerton.

A note included in the official documents for the Cause states, 'Angram Grange, now Ingram Grange, in the parish of Welbury, North Riding of Yorkshire. That it was from here that Bowes came, and not from Angram Grange in Coxwold parish, as has sometimes been supposed, is definitely established by the legal enquiry after the martyr's execution. Ingram Grange was formerly a grange or outlying farm belonging to the Cistercian Abbey of Rievaulx and was leased to the Bowes family in 1554 (Victoria County History, North Riding, II, p. 81). It is a few miles from the village of Appleton Wiske in the district of Cleveland, (a large hilly district in the North Riding)'.

Marmaduke Bowes was distantly related to the great Bowes family of the North, but the precise connection is not clear. His date of birth is unknown, but his father's will of 1570 gives the information that Marmaduke was the eldest of six children and that he was already married with four children of his own. Marmaduke Bowes is called a 'gentleman' by Lady Babthorpe. The Chalcedon Catalogue calls him a 'noble layman'. Father John Mush describes him as 'an honest substantial gentleman or yeoman, I know not certainly which'.

But it is Father Mush who provides the most valuable information about Marmaduke Bowes. This priest was living in York at the time of the arrest and therefore in a position to have accurate information. He put it all in writing within three to six months of the execution. And he took a special interest in the case because of its close relationship with the martyrdom of St Margaret Clitherow.

Father Mush was not just one of the priests associated with Margaret Clitherow's Mass centre in the Shambles at York. He was her close friend and spiritual director. He was a man of vehemence who expressed himself strongly, and when Margaret was martyred only four months after the martyrdom of Marmaduke Bowes, he made the special point that injustice from Bowes's trial had had its effect in Margaret's trial.

Marmaduke Bowes, when he appeared before the Council of the North, had been convicted on the unsupported word of one witness. John Mush claimed that the Council had been reprimanded by one of the Assize Judges for having condemned Bowes unjustly, and in retaliation the Council had contrived to have an Assize Judge condemn Margaret on similar unsupported evidence in order to prove their point.

In pursuit of his claim of injustice, Father Mush gave great prominence to Marmaduke Bowes when he wrote his account of the Life and Martyrdom of Margaret Clitherow, and the Middlesbrough Diocese is fortunate to possess the Middleton manuscript, which can be dated to 1586 and is the earliest known copy of this work. This is what Father Mush says about Marmaduke Bowes: 'He was wonderfully beloved and well spoken of among his neighbours, one that liked well of the Catholic religion, as in heart believing it to be the infallible and only true religion of

God . . . yet fearing, as infinite do, the extremity of these late monstrous laws and statutes which most unnaturally do oppress and violate the natural liberty of man's conscience . . . he chose rather some times to accompany the ministers and to go into their church than he would fall to the unmerciful handlings of heretics and lose both goods and liberty. Thus he continued a long time, divided miserably within himself, detesting all their heresies in his heart and yet fearing in his bodily actions to show himself a Catholic, believing inwardly the Catholic faith in every point, and yet fearing not to seem outwardly a heretic. Nevertheless in all this time of his schismatical dissemblings, he thought it a desperate point of impiety to shut up his hospitality from priests, whom he knew well to be messengers of God . . . and to these men, I say, he opened his doors bountifully'.

Father Mush is describing a very typical Catholic layman of these troubled times, when England had no Catholic Bishop and very few priests and the individual could receive very little guidance from authority. At first lay people had to make their own decisions in isolation and safety seemed to justify pretence. Many obeyed the law and went to the Anglican Church while remaining at heart true Catholics, and modern critics should be slow to condemn the sincere actions of devout men and women who with the best intentions in the world made the wrong decisions. Lady Babthorpe could call Marmaduke Bowes, 'no Catholic, but a good schismatic'; modern historians would call him a 'Church Papist'.

True to his interior convictions, Marmaduke Bowes employed a Catholic tutor for his children. This man, Martin Harrison, according to Father Mush, 'was sadly apprehended in the bishoprick (County Durham), as I remember, by John Barnes, brother to the false bishop about Whitsunday, 1585'. By cruelty, threats and bribery, the tutor was induced to give up his Faith and then required to return to his employer's house to act as a spy for the Government.

In due time, Martin Harrison produced evidence against Marmaduke Bowes for harbouring priests, and the martyr and his wife were summoned to York. They were in prison for a short time and then released on bond to await the next gaol delivery. Charges against Mrs Bowes were apparently dropped but her husband remained on bond. When Father Hugh Taylor was arrested 'in another man's house', Marmaduke Bowes must have been relieved that the arrest had not been made in his own house where Father Taylor had been harboured many times before.

Perhaps news of the arrest reached Angram Grange, and Mr Bowes took horse at once for York to defend his friend, or perhaps it was all a matter of bad luck and Mr Bowes arrived in York to answer to his bond at the very time that Father Taylor was on trial. Certainly, the connection between Father Taylor and Mr Bowes was known to the court, and the layman was charged specifically with harbouring Father Taylor. Father Mush laments that Mr Bowes 'was indicted and condemned upon only evidence of the schoolmaster who had broken his Faith and promise to God and man a little before, still carrying a conscience saleable for sixpence, of known and notable infamy, as it was openly reported before the bench, and proved against him'.

The Council of the North found Marmaduke Bowes guilty of contravening the Statute of Queen Elizabeth 'against Jesuits, seminary priests and such other like disobedient persons', and he was condemned to death. He was the first layman in the country to suffer under this Statute. In prison, awaiting execution, Marmaduke Bowes made his full submission to the Catholic Church, and it seems probable that he was reconciled by Father Taylor. Father Mush reports, 'he boldly confessed with great alacrity of mind, lamenting that he had lived in schism so long, and without fear of death desired not to live any longer, but that his death might be some part of satisfaction for his schismatical dissembling past, and in the mercy of Christ, who made full satisfaction for us all, he offered up his own life, wishing that he had many more to spend in so good a cause'.

As he was not a priest, Marmaduke Bowes was not hanged, drawn and quartered, but was simply hanged in York on 27 November, 1585.

Francis Ingleby

The Ingleby family of Ripley Castle in the West Riding was a most determined recusant family. The Earl of Huntingdon, President of the Council of the North, called them 'a nest of traitors', and in 1572 committed himself more politely to the statement that this family was one of the strongest supports of Catholicism in Yorkshire. The head of the family, Sir William, was in fact an occasional conformist and a true son of his times, who ensured that his wife and children should be openly recusant while he tried to protect his property by subterfuge.

Sir William and Lady Anne Ingleby had a family of six sons and eight daughters. Their fourth son was Francis, the future martyr, who was born at Ripley Castle about the year 1550.

The Catholic life of the family must have had a profound influence on Francis. No doubt he could appreciate his father's position, but his mother, Lady Anne, was a woman of deep faith and great courage. Between 1571 and 1581, she was summoned to appear before the Council of the North twenty-seven times, but each time she sent feeble excuses or just failed to put in an appearance.

The family was distantly related to the Ingleby family of Hutton Rudby in the North Riding, but it was not until 1593 that the name of the first Ingleby of Hutton Rudby appears on the recusant roll, and by 1633 they had sold their Hutton Rudby estates and settled at Lawkland and Ripon.

Francis Ingleby spent his childhood at or around Ripley Castle, and then about 1562 entered Brasenose College in the University of Oxford, but there is no mention of his obtaining a degree. By 1577, he was studying Law at the Inner Temple.

When his father died in 1579, he left his son an annuity of £20 to be paid from the family estates until such time as he qualified as a barrister and was able to earn his living.

But Francis had other ideas. According to Father Richard Holtby SJ (in Grene's Collection E) the priestly vocation was suggested to him by one of his friends, William Pullain, when they were walking together in London, and Francis considered the proposal very carefully. He accepted the fact that with so many brothers it was only fitting that one of them should consecrate himself to God as a priest and work for the larger family of the English Catholics, and many times he seemed to hear a voice saying to him, 'Arise and set forth'.

On 18 August, 1582, the Douai Dairy records the arrival at Rheims of Francis Ingleby as a student for the priesthood. His ecclesiastical course was short and rapid. He was ordained subdeacon in May 1583, deacon in September 1583, and on 17 December 1583 was ordained to the priesthood at Laon. On 5 April 1584 he set out for the English Mission. There can be no doubt that he came immediately to the city of York. Dr Anthony Champney records (about 1618) with due discretion, 'his fruitful labours in the northern parts of England', but Father Ingleby achieved so much in York in such a short time that he could not have been based anywhere else. For two years, he lived in a city where the City Fathers were determined to stamp out every trace of the Catholic religion and where the Catholics were organising themselves in powerful resistance.

Father Ingleby arrived in York at a time when there were too many priests in the city for safety's sake and security was lax. There were too many arrests and too many Catholic prisoners. Each priest was working as an individual, and there was no authority to direct or co-ordinate their activities. Priests tended to live in the private residences of Catholic gentry, where they were safe, and inevitably the needs of many poorer Catholics were overlooked. In these circumstances, leadership was desperately required, and a little after 1583 Cardinal Allen had appointed Father John Mush as a leader to whom he seems to have delegated a certain amount of authority, but it was not until 1584–5 that progress was made.

J.C.H. Aveling, the modern historical expert on these affairs, has written in *Catholic Recusancy in York*, (p. 71): 'In 1584–5, there was a considerable ordering of the seminary priests' mission in the north by Richard Holtby SJ and John Mush, who had special faculties to direct priests. Priests were organised into small groups of two or three, each with a large mission area. They were to be itinerant, touring their areas in the guise of travelling dealers. Normally, they were to have no residences, but only rest houses, sited in deserted places in the country'. Aveling goes on to state that York and the Ainstey formed one such district and was taken over by Father Mush himself with Father Thomas Bell as his assistant, and that within a few months Father Francis Ingleby replaced Father Bell. St Margaret Clitherow's 'hide' in the Shambles played its part in this plan, and would house one or two priests at a time on their brief and irregularly spaced visits to the City.

Father Ingleby was well known to St Margaret Clitherow. Mary Claridge, her biographer, refers to him as Margaret Clitherow's confessor.

Father Ingleby's two years in York were filled with incident, excitement and danger. The Government was exerting special pressure; priests were being captured. Everyone was talking about the trials and subsequent deaths of Father Hugh Taylor and Mr Marmaduke Bowes. The Authorities knew all about Margaret Clitherow's activities and were about to pounce.

The Mass house in the Shambles was raided on 10 March, 1586. No priest was found, only a Catholic schoolmaster, Mr Stapleton, teaching the children. But it was enough. The vestments and altar materials were taken away, Margaret arrested once more, and the little Flemish boy began to talk.

News was brought to Margaret Clitherow in prison that the Flemish boy had accused her of harbouring several priests, and two were mentioned by name: Mr Francis Ingleby of Rheims and Mr John Mush of Rome. Margaret knew that the lives of Father Mush and Father Ingleby depended on her silence.

By a legal technicality, the names of the priests could not be mentioned in the indictment, and it is said that one of the reasons why Margaret refused to make any plea at all and thus indirectly caused her own death was to make sure that no priest's name was mentioned. But now the hunt was really on for John Mush and

Francis Ingleby and both tried to disappear completely from view. Mush was fortunate; he got clean away. Ingleby preserved his liberty for three months but was then captured in unfortunate circumstances.

There are three differing accounts of his arrest, but all agree in outline. The first is an unsigned document of 1590 in Father Christopher Grene's Collection of Documents E. On the evidence of modern handwriting experts it is attributed to Father Richard Holtby. This relates that on 28 May 1586 Francis Ingleby, dressed as a poor countryman, was waiting to cross the river Ouse in York, when a Catholic nobleman, William Lacey, recognised him and removed his hat as a mark of respect to the priest. They stayed talking for a little while, but unfortunately the place where they stood was overlooked by the windows of the palace of the Protestant Archbishop, and Mr Henry Cheke, Secretary to the Council of the North, happened to look out of one of these windows and thought it very suspicious that a nobleman should be showing such respect to a man so poorly dressed. He acted on his suspicions and hauled them both in for examination.

The second account is in Father Christopher Grene's Collection M. This paper cannot be accurately dated and the author is unknown, but it was probably written about 1590. It states, 'Mr Francis Ingleby, son to Sir William Ingleby, Knight, having occasion to go to York, a Catholic gentleman by name Mr Lassie (Lacey) met him in a place called Bishopfields . . . and kneeling down craved his blessing . . . which being espied by one of the President's men . . . he was taken . . . and brought to the Council'. It goes on to relate, 'They said unto him that they marvelled . . . that he being a gentleman of so great calling would abase himself to be a priest. He answered that he made more account of his priesthood than of all other titles whatsoever'.

From this same account there is further detail of his imprisonment: 'Brought unto the Castle, he had a pair of fetters laid upon his legs at the prison door. With a smiling countenance, he said, "I fear me I shall be overproud of my new boots," meaning his fetters'.

The third account is very similar to the first and is found again in Father Christopher Grene's Collection M. The original was written by Father William Warford SJ, and is endorsed by Father Robert Parsons SJ. It states that Father Ingleby was leaving York, on foot and in disguise. Suspicions were aroused when his companion showed too many marks of respect to a traveller so poorly dressed. The chaplains to the Protestant Archbishop noticed this, made enquiries and had the priest arrested.

Father Francis Ingleby was brought to trial before the Council of the North on 2 June 1586. His judges were the Vice-President, Sir Thomas Fairfax, Mr Henry Cheke, and Mr Ralph Hurlestone or Huddlestone. All official records of the trial have been lost, but from Catholic sources it is clear that he was charged under the Statute of 1585, 'against Jesuits, seminary priests and such other like disobedient persons'.

A Catholic document of 1586 in Father Christopher Grene's Collection E is quite explicit. It was possibly written by Father John Mush and certainly reflects his forthright attitude and powerful expression. It states unequivocally that Francis Ingleby was condemned and murdered as a traitor solely because he was a priest of Rheims. This document also describes the difficulties of his trial: 'With him, they used such guileful dealing, that they might entangle him with an oath to disclose in what Catholic men's houses he had been harboured, but they could not deceive him. When he was about to speak anything, they stopped him with railing and blasphemies, overthwarting him in every word and interrupting him by one frivolous question after another, that before he had answered two words to one matter, they came upon him with another, in so much that many noted how they would not suffer him to make a perfect end of any one sentence'.

Father Ingleby was found guilty and condemned to death. He was taken back to the Castle to await his execution, but the Catholics of York changed his pathetic procession into a triumphal way. They leaned out of their windows and shouted for his blessing as he passed by. And according to another anonymous document in Father Christopher Grene's Collection M, he blessed them privately, saying all the time, 'Oh sweet judgement'. The same document continues: 'After his condemnation, he showed such tokens of inward joy that the keeper, named Mr Neverall, said that he took no small pleasure to behold his sweet and joyful conversation . . . for his joy was such that the keeper, a very earnest Puritan, could not abstain from tears'.

Next day, the priest was dragged on a hurdle through the streets of York to the Knavesmire. There is evidence that large crowds watched him pass by, but the Catholics could only watch from a distance. One young man in the crowd got himself into trouble by uttering indiscreet words. For this he was reported and the way began for his own martyrdom. His name was Robert Bickerdike. He was to be martyred within three months.

At the Knavesmire, Father Ingleby was subjected to the importunities of a Protestant minister, by name Mr Frost, but as Father Thomas Stanney SJ explained (1609), 'All was in vain, for he utterly condemned his speeches and with great constancy and alacrity submitted himself to the torments of death'.

Father William Warford SJ, who knew Francis Ingleby personally, has left this description of him: 'He was a man of short stature but well built. He seemed about thirty five years of age or thereabouts. He was of light complexion, wore a chestnut beard and had a slight cast in his eyes. He was sharp and quick in mind, ready and facile in speech, austere and grave in countenance, and assiduous in action. Yorkshire suffered a great loss in his death for he was most highly esteemed by all Catholics on account of his great zeal for souls and especially on account of his remarkable prudence'.

Father Francis Ingleby was hanged, drawn and quartered at York on 3 June, 1586.

John Fingley

Barmby in the Marsh is the little village in Howdenshire where the waters of the Derwent flow into the Ouse. Surrounded by the rich farm lands of drained marsh and hemmed in by the rivers the place is isolated, but being close to Hemingbrough, once one of the richest parishes in England, and less than three miles from Howden, where the Bishops of Durham had their residence in former times, the people of the village were kept in touch with the larger world. They were well served in Catholic times by the visiting vicar of the Barmby Prebend in Howden Minster and they enjoyed the kindly patronage of the powerful Babthorpe family from their manor at Babthorpe across the fields.

Here in Barmby, in 1553, a second son was born to John Fingley, a yeoman, and his wife Elizabeth, and the Parish Registers of Howden Minister record that the baby was christened John on 7 November 1553. Queen Mary had just been crowned in the previous month, so for his first five years only could the child have been educated as a Catholic before the accession of Queen Elizabeth brought religious turmoil.

The boy's father died in 1570, when John was seventeen years of age, but despite this loss and the poverty of his family, the opportunities of those days were such that his scholastic abilities were recognised and he secured admission to Cambridge University where he matriculated in 1573 as a member of Gonville and Caius College. His status was that of a sizar, i.e. a poor student who received free lodging and tuition in return for certain menial services.

John Fingley was fortunate in his choice of College. It had been founded as recently as 1557 by John Caius, one of the leading physicians of his day, and received its first statutes in the same year as a result of the Visitation of the University made by Cardinal Pole as Papal Legate and Bishop Scott, Master of Christ's College. But the life of Gonville and Caius as a Catholic College was very short. The following year, Queen Elizabeth came to the throne and the whole University was subjected to Protestant pressures.

John Caius managed to retain the Mastership of the College he had founded, and preserved a Catholic influence. At Court, he was recognised as a Catholic and for this reason dismissed from his position as personal physician to the Queen in 1568, but he remained at the head of his College until his death in 1573. His successor as Master was another man with strong Catholic sympathies, Dr Thomas Legge, and for the next thirty years under his Mastership the College seems to have been especially congenial to Catholics.

Archbishop Maurice Couve de Murville and Mr Philip Jenkins in their recent book on Catholic Cambridge have collected evidence of a Catholic presence in a Protestant College, and follow J. Venn's conclusions (in *Early Collegiate Life*, published 1913) that a considerable number of Caius men became priests abroad after leaving. Among them were Father Richard Holtby SJ of York and John Fingley.

There is no evidence that John Fingley was a Catholic before entering Caius College; but then there is no evidence that he was not. At first he was the personal servant to Hugh Cressy, one of the Fellows, but in a very short time was appointed personal servant to the Master himself, and Dr Legge thought so highly of him that he promoted him to the prestigious office of Butler of the College in 1574.

For three years all was peaceful. John Fingley continued his studies and was obviously in close contact with the Master who was at least suspected to be a Catholic. This caused considerable unrest in the College especially from 1577 as anti-Catholic feeling grew, and in 1581 a major row developed. The details of this confrontation are given in the Lansdowne Manuscript in the British Library, and they are recounted by J. Venn in the Caian, vol I p. 169 and vol 5 p. 152. The Fellows of the College complained that the Master and Richard Swale, the President, were both too favourably inclined towards Catholics, and they seized on John Fingley's appointment as College Butler as a case in point. They claimed that this ancient office was so important that it should be filled only by the Master and Fellows as a corporate body and not by the Master acting independently. In fact when these complaints were made, John Fingley had already left the College, but the statements made about him are illuminating. He was described as 'an arrant papist' and 'a great perverter of youth'. It was said that he never came to common prayer or sermons. It was stated that one of the reasons why another student, Robert Sayre (who was later ordained priest in Rome and joined the Benedictines) was refused a degree was that he had been 'of great and familiar acquaintance with Fingley, a pernicious papist'. Finally, it was claimed that it had been rumoured in the College that Fingley was already a priest and that he had even said Mass in 'the Master's greater chamber over the parlour'.

The Lansdowne Manuscript makes it very clear that John Fingley had been forced to leave Cambridge without a degree. It insists that he was not 'sent away by the Master', but 'his lewd dealing being detected, he ran away for fear of further punishment by others'.

John Fingley arrived at Rheims and was admitted to the English College on 13 February 1580. His studies for the priesthood were brief; he was obviously no theological beginner. He was ordained priest on Holy Saturday, 25 March 1581, in Our Lady's Church, Rheims, by the Bishop of Châlons-sur-Marne. He followed the custom of the time and delayed his first Mass until 3 April, but three weeks after this he set sail for England to begin his missionary work.

Very little is known about John Fingley's work as a priest. He must have been successful because he was not caught for four years and that was a very long time for a priest to preserve his freedom in the England of those days. The Douai Diary says he laboured in the northern parts of the country. Modern historians can be no more exact. J.C.H. Aveling says he worked in the north of England; Father Godfrey Anstruther says he apparently worked in Yorkshire. It was customary for most missionary priests of the time to work in their own home regions where they knew the land and knew the people, and John Fingley's presence in Howdenshire would not be a rash speculation. After all, his mother was still living in Barmby, and there were many active Catholics in the district.

Nothing is known about the details of John Fingley's arrest, except that it must have taken place before the end of June 1585. He was taken to York and put in Peter Prison, which Father John A. Myerscough SJ claims was situated on the very site on which now stands St Wilfrid's Catholic Church. (*The Martyrs of Durham*, p. 68).

In this prison, Father Fingley had a strange encounter with one of the many valiant Catholic women of his day. This was Miss Frances Webster, the details of whose story have been preserved by Father Christopher Grene SJ in his Collection of Documents F. The source of this information is an original paper of unknown authorship but from its contents it would seem to have been written in the 1590's. According to this paper, a certain Arthur Webster obtained a commission 'for the attacking of papists', and then used his official powers to arrest his mother, Mrs Margaret Webster, and his sister, Miss Frances Webster, who were both well known as Catholics.

The young girl was 'set alone in Peter's prison at York . . . (she) showed herself most constant, a bold confessor of Christ's Catholic doctrine, fervent, zealous, devout, patient, quiet, charitable, never ceasing to work good works with all her power.

'For when a priest of God was put into a low prison under her, into a deep and darksome dungeon, this blessed maiden found the means to open a grate and to let in some light unto him in the darkness'.

'But, O God, how joyful a heart had he, [in the margin: Mr John Fingley] when he beheld her constancy . . . when he heard her comforting speeches . . . when he experienced also her true charity.

'For she obtained him a gown for the clothing of his body during the day and to stand him in place of a bed for the night.

'And when she was examined for this work of mercy, she boldly answered that she had given it, and that if it were to give, she would give it and show any work of mercy to the annointed of God'.

The condition of the prison in which they were both confined does not bear description. How long Frances Webster had been there is not known but her health was already badly affected. She was removed to York Castle to join her mother, and she died there on 29 June 1585.

Father John Fingley was brought to trial at York, probably at the Summer Assizes of 1586. No official records of the trial have survived, but Father William Harewell had access to the York Assize Register in about 1628 when he was compiling the Paris Catalogue, and from this authority, he states that the priest had to answer three charges:

1. that he had come into England after being ordained overseas;
2. that he had declared the Queen to be a heretic;
3. that he had reconciled Frances Webster to the Catholic Church.

Each of these charges was a capital offence, and Father John Fingley was found guilty of High Treason and condemned to death.

Father John Mullen, an Irish secular priest, wrote in 1629 that Father Fingley 'suffered with that generosity characteristic of the seminary priest from the very beginning and with that ardour for the confirmation of religion'. Father Anthony Champney, a fellow Yorkshireman who knew the martyr well, said that when John Fingley was very young in Barmby, his death by hanging had been foretold to his mother, and that unless he was mistaken Mrs Fingley was present at her son's execution.

John Fingley was hanged, drawn and quartered at York on 8 August, 1586.

Robert Bickerdike

The city of York in 1585 was not the safest part of the country for Catholics to live in. The High Commission sweep of 1580–1581 was over but the consequent arrests and imprisonments had weakened the recusant body and many Catholics had been forced to give up their Faith and conform to the Established Church. Nevertheless, as J.C.H. Aveling (*Catholic Recusancy in York*, pp. 65–66) has pointed out, there was still a small but resolute group of Catholics in the city and the work of reorganisation was under way. Government pressure was now directed more and more towards the lay Catholics rather than the priests, as Father John Mush has suggested 'for want of priests'.

Among the lay Catholics so honoured was Robert Bickerdike. He was a 'young man from a noble family' according to the Chalcedon Returns of 1626, and elsewhere in those Returns Father Ralph Fisher calls him a gentleman. He had been born at Low Hall, in the parish of Farnham, near Knaresbrough, but had moved to York at an early age to serve his apprenticeship. He was closely related to Robert Maskew, a grocer, who had been Lord Mayor of York in 1574 and was still on the City Council in 1585. His family were well known in York and some of them at least were recusants, but Robert Bickerdike himself may not always have persisted in the faith. The Chalcedon Returns describe him as one 'who had been reconciled to the Catholic Church' but this statement may be based on Government sources and could mean as little as the reception of the sacrament of Confession.

By 1585, Robert Bickerdike was obviously a very convinced Catholic who did not hesitate to proclaim his religion openly even to the point of indiscretion. He was well known as a Catholic and was first arrested in this year when he was seen in the company of a known Catholic priest, Father (now Saint) John Boste. A document of 1586 (possibly written by Father John Mush) in Father Christopher Grene's Collection E reports that he was arrested 'because they were seen drinking together and the heretics surmised that this young man paid for the pot of ale, which they thought was matter sufficient to hang him'. Father John Boste was too experienced as a fugitive to be captured lightly and he promptly escaped his captors and was able to continue his ministry for another eight years before paying the penalty for his Priesthood at Durham in 1593. Robert Bickerdike alone was put in prison.

According to one document, Bickerdike appeared at the Quarter Sessions at the Guildhall, York, on 23 July 1858, and was charged under the statute of the same year 'against Jesuits, seminary priests and such other like disobedient persons'. This indictment is still in existence in the York City Archives and states quite clearly that John Boste was accused of coming into England as a Catholic priest ordained overseas and that Robert Bickerdike was accused of giving him assistance. All this is very strange because Quarter Sessions had no jurisdiction over capital offences and certainly John Boste was not in custody at the time. 'This indictment', wrote J.C.H. Aveling (*Catholic Recusancy in York*, p. 204) 'is a mystery, since it was not proceeded with and in form (e.g. the date given) is bogus'.

This official document may be confusing but contemporary Catholic sources collected by Father Christopher Grene confirm that Robert Bickerdike was certainly arrested at this time and put on trial, and it is possibly Father John Mush who adds the information that a second charge of speaking treasonable words to another apprentice was added: 'This young man, Bickerdike, had many malicious merchants of York his enemies, for he had served as an apprentice there and was known to be Catholically affected. Amongst which was one Brooke and Andrew Trewe, two as malicious as ignorant Puritans. By the means and envious procurements of these and their accomplices, he was at his first taking arraigned in the Common Hall in York, and indicted . . . for saying to an heretical apprentice . . . that he might now say his pleasure, for the sap is with the Catholics in the root of the tree, but yet may perhaps ascend upwards towards Michaelmas and then he would use no such railing words'. (Father John Mush (?) in Grene's Collection E).

Bickerdike's words may have been harmless enough and he himself explained them in an innocent way, but they were taken to be a reference to the projected Spanish invasion and consequently a threat to Queen and Government.

The members of the jury for the first trial were not impressed by the evidence produced and Robert Bickerdike was acquitted. He was not released, however, but despite his proven innocence was returned to prison to await the next Assizes to be tried a second time for the same offences.

This second trial took place at the Summer Assizes in the Guildhall in 1586. All official records of these Assizes have been lost but there remains much contemporary Catholic evidence. The account attributed to Father John Mush describes how Clench and Rodes, sitting as Judges of the Bench, questioned Bickerdike about the previous charges. Bickerdike replied that he had been cleared of these charges a year before. They then tried to trick him with the famous 'bloody' question. What would he do if England were invaded by the Pope. Would he support the Pope or his Queen? On this point, Bickerdike refused to commit himself and replied very wisely that 'he could not tell in time before, what he would do in time to come. But, quoth he, I will do as it shall please God to put me in mind'.

At this the Judges insulted him and called him a traitor, but were so vehement in their denunciations that they defeated their own purposes and their malice only served to shock the members of the jury, who at once declared the prisoner not guilty as charged. Once more Robert Bickerdike should have been freed as an innocent man but once more the course of justice was perverted, and the Judges ordered that he should be returned to the Ousebridge prison until such time as they could instruct Martin Birkhead, the Queen's Attorney, to prepare a better case.

The third trial was a special sitting of the Assizes. The same Judges presided; only the jury was different. The Judges, who had assured Bickerdike at the end of the previous trial that 'he would not escape them', now began by instructing the new jury on their duty to convict. 'This traitor had too favourable and too scrupulous a jury in the town, but I trust you will look otherwise to him, being the Queen's enemy and a notorious traitor'. Such were the opening words of Judge Rodes.

There is some confusion about the precise nature of the charges preferred against Robert Bickerdike. One account says he was accused as before of harbouring Father John Boste and speaking treasonable words. Another account maintains he was accused only of speaking treasonable words but quotes the 'sap in the root of the tree' in completely different circumstances. Another cites his reply to the 'bloody question'. William Hutton, a Catholic draper in York, has left a document (preserved in the Stoneyhurst manuscripts, Anglia VI, p. 46) in which he suggests that Robert Bickerdike was also on trial for an indiscreet remark he had made to the wife of a Protestant minister. According to this William Hutton, Robert Bickerdike had been in the crowd watching Father Francis Ingleby dragged to his martyrdom, when he overhead this lady calling the priest 'a treacherous thief'. With more courage than discretion, the impetuous young man contradicted her flatly. 'No. No thief', he said 'but as true as you are'. The lady reported him to her husband and he used all the influence he could muster to bring Bickerdike to trial for using seditious words.

From all this, it would seem that Robert Bickerdike was accused of a variety of 'crimes', all of them associated with his religion and all carrying in some way the penalty of death. Perhaps the most reliable information about the main charge has been provided in a remarkable way from the long lost records of the York Assize Register. These were still in existence and at the disposal of Father William Harewell, (alias Farrar and Gray) when in 1628 he was composing his Paris Catalogue of Martyrs, and from these official Government documents he takes the statement that Robert Bickerdike was condemned under the 1581 statute of Queen Elizabeth that decreed that any Englishman reconciled to the Church of Rome was guilty of High Treason and should be put to death by the process of being hanged, drawn and quartered.

In fact, Robert Bickerdike was hanged, drawn and quartered as conviction under this statute would have demanded. If he had been convicted under the statute of 1585 'against Jesuits, seminary priests and such like disobedient persons', he would have been deemed guilty of a felony only, because he was a layman and not a priest, and the penalty for this was death by hanging without being drawn and quartered.

The shameful treatment accorded to Bickerdike at his trial was continued in prison while he awaited death. The Sheriffs of the city stole the gold ring from his finger and took away all his money and his clothes, and the indignation of the local Catholics is clearly reflected in contemporary accounts.

He was allowed some visitors in the death cell, and among them was his sister, Mrs Bridget Maskew, who was herself a valiant Confessor of the Faith and spent many years of her life in prison for her religion. In a paper of 1590, probably written by Father Richard Holtby SJ, (Grene's Collection E) it is stated that it was Mrs Maskew who provided new clothes for her brother so that he was dressed properly and becomingly in white when the time came for him to meet his Heavenly Father. This was a practice much developed in later years when the Catholic friends of a martyr would club together to buy new white clothes for those about to die for Christ.

Robert Bickerdike was hanged, drawn and quartered at York in late August, 1586. The exact date of his martyrdom cannot be determined. The date of 23 July has been suggested by several contemporaries but this is too early: the Lammas Assizes at which he was condemned could not begin until 1 August.

The paper of 1586, in Grene's Collection E, (Father John Mush (?)) provides a fitting postscript to the life and death of young Robert Bickerdike. This states, 'All the country was amazed to see this young man so unjustly made away with, and some gentlemen being in company with (Judge) Rodes before he departed from Yorkshire, asked him whether the young man's answer (that he would do in time to come as it should please God to put into his mind) was treason by any statute or law or no. Which demand, Rodes took in great dudgeon and said: you do us no less injury than the traitor did at the bar, when he asked us the same question'. And the learned Judge then added the remark: 'We are not sent here to scan and dispute the statutes but to give judgement against offenders'.

Alexander Crowe

'How say you to one that was first a cobbler, then a porter, after that under-cook in the Seminary and at last by his extreme diligence got as much learning as was sufficient for a priest, and finally such favour at God's hands to be a martyr?' So wrote the Douai priest, Dr Humphrey Ely, in 1603 about Alexander Crowe.

Humphrey Ely was a convert clergyman from the diocese of Hereford, and had been Vicar of Ugborough in Devon in 1571. Later he crossed the seas to Douai, became a Catholic and was ordained priest. He spent the rest of his life quietly teaching law first at the University of Douai and then at the University of Pont-à-Mousson. He appears to have taken little part in the Catholic controversies of the day until his indignation was aroused by a book of Father Robert Persons SJ which was published in 1601.

In this book, Father Persons seemed to refer disparagingly to seminary priests and looked down on them because some of them had previously been serving men or soldiers. Dr Ely's reply was to quote Alexander Crowe the cobbler and James Clayton, the smith. 'Serving men, yea,' he writes, 'and of mean quality, but who have come by their zeal and constancy to the height of perfection, which is martyrdom'. He concludes, 'Go now and object to that worthy priest of pious and famous memory, Cardinal Allen, that he made not only serving men and soldiers priests, but also cobblers and smiths'.

Alexander Crowe was indeed a cobbler, possibly in Howden, certainly in York. His date of birth has been calculated as being about 1550. Father William Warford SJ, who knew him at Douai, says he was thirty-six in 1587.

In the Chalcedon Returns of 1626, Bishop Richard Smith quotes the testimony of Mrs Elizabeth Ellison, who was living at Cliffe near Hemingbrough in 1604. She states, 'Mr Alexander Crowe was born at South Duffield, (some say Howden) in Yorkshire'. But the Bishop himself states categorically that Crowe was born in Howden, and we have his own assurance in the Preface to his work that he checked details of this sort very carefully and never accepted doubtful information as certain.

The Parish Registers of Howden Minster go back to 1542 but have no record of his baptism. The Registers of Hemingbrough, in which parish South Duffield is situated, go back only to 1605. Father Godfrey Anstruther OP, the modern authority on the seminary priests, accepts Howden as the birthplace of Alexander Crowe on the evidence of Chalcedon, and acknowledges that he later went to York. The official Documents of the Cause state, 'Alexander Crowe was born in the East Riding of Yorkshire most probably in the parish of Howden.'

As a Catholic shoemaker in York, Alexander Crowe would have many contacts with the seminary priests, and hearing that they were short of servants in the seminary at Rheims, he offered his services and began his duties there in 1581, when he was about thirty-one years of age.

Just when he recognised his vocation to the priesthood is too personal a matter to be formally recorded. Perhaps he left York with the priesthood in mind; perhaps he thought about it only while working in Rheims. Certainly it can have been no easy decision for a man completely lacking in education and one is left with the uneasy feeling that this unusual cobbler must have applied himself to his studies before he ever left York and that he went to Rheims with only one purpose in mind: the priesthood.

The transition from cobbler to priest took two years and eight months. Is it possible to move from illiteracy to theological competence in such time? But Alexander Crowe arrived on 30 April 1581 and was ordained on 17 December 1583. His companion, Father William Warford SJ, describes how he worked as a servant in the College before beginning his studies for the priesthood, and Dr Humphrey Ely is even more explicit, stating, 'by his virtue and exemplary patience and by his modesty and humility, he earned the right to be admitted to the study of letters, and ultimately to be promoted to the priesthood'. After his ordination, Father Alexander Crowe remained in Rheims for another two months before setting out for the English mission on 27 February 1584. But his time as a priest was even shorter than his time of preparation. The conditions in England at the time were such that he lasted but eighteen months.

Of his apostolate very little is known. He would seem to have worked in the East Riding and particularly in Howdenshire. His contemporary Mrs Elizabeth Ellison of Cliffe states that 'after he had worked here some time with much edification to all who knew him, he was taken at South Duffield. . .' (Chalcedon Returns 1626). She is obviously referring to her own district of Cliffe in Howdenshire and the people she knew who knew him as a priest.

Father Richard Holtby SJ gives us a glimpse of him as 'a man burning with zeal for souls, who therefore never refused any labour by which he could win them', and adds later that he usually travelled round on foot. (Grene's Collection E, 1590). Father William Warford SJ describes him as a 'simple man but with a wonderful zeal for souls, so that he could not be held back or deterred by any dangers. . . He was of more than medium height, with a serious countenance and black beard, well built and with a strong physique'.

Father Crowe was arrested while actively engaged on his priestly duties. Towards the end of 1586, he was summoned at night to South Duffield, to minister to a Catholic woman, Cecily Garnett, who was having a baby. Possibly he was caught in a trap, for South Duffield was known as a stronghold of Catholics, and it was also well known to all in those days when many babies died at birth that it was a Catholic custom for the priest to the summoned as soon as a birth was imminent so that he could baptise the baby as soon as possible. A known Catholic woman about to give birth would certainly be watched very closely by informers in the hope of catching the priest. In this case, their vigil was rewarded and Father Crowe was taken before the local Justice of the Peace to be examined, and when he admitted that he was a Catholic priest, he was brought before the Council of the North at York, and committed to prison.

In Father Christopher Grene's Collection E, there is another paper, dated 1586 and probably written by Father John Mush, and in this, some of the details of Father Crowe's sufferings have been preserved, including the information that he was put in double fetters in among the criminals. Another paper of the same time, probably written by Father Richard Holtby SJ, adds that conditions in the prison were so bad that Father Crowe picked up a fever which stayed with him until death.

Both accounts converge to give a vivid picture of Father Crowe's trial. At the height of his fever, he was violently dragged from the bed on which he lay and brought into court before the Council of the North. Despite his illness he had prepared well for his trial. As he left prison he was carrying in his hands a small wooden cross which he had made himself, but the gaolers snatched it from him and broke it into pieces. He had also prepared himself by shaving the crown of his head in a priestly tonsure so that rather than attempting to disguise his priesthood he was openly proclaiming it to all.

The judges, Sir William Mallory, Laurence Mears, Ralph Hurlstone and George Gibson, were angered by his defiance and throughout the trial mocked him and ridiculed him, trying in every way by lies and slanders to make him an object of scorn and derision for the people. Nor was the case of Father Crowe helped by the entry into the court room of another Catholic prisoner, the future lay martyr, Blessed Richard Langley. This elderly Catholic gentleman from Ousethorpe near Pocklington was surprised to recognise a priest in court, and immediately threw himself on his knees before Father Crowe and piously asked for his blessing.

Having admitted his priesthood and openly flaunted it, Alexander Crowe had no hope of acquittal. By his own admission he had broken the statute of 1585 'against Jesuits, seminary priests and such other like disobedient persons' and as such was guilty of high treason. The judges sentenced him to be hanged, drawn and quartered and he was returned to prison to await death.

The *Historia Particular de la Persecucion de Inglaterra* is a valuable source of information on Father Alexander Crowe. It was written in 1599 by Diego de Yepes, Bishop of Tarragona in Spain, but was compiled from material supplied by Father Joseph Creswell SJ, Rector of the English College Rome from 1589 to 1592 and later resident in Spain. The book belongs to Creswell rather than Yepes and a contemporary has said it has nothing of Yepes except his name. It is this book that describes the way in which Father Crowe reacted to the chill news that he was to die. 'He began to be greatly comforted and to show such great joy to the court that all those present took notice of it, and returning to the prison, he could not contain himself all that day, so great was his satisfaction at the thought that he was to die on the morrow'.

But perhaps the greatest value of this Spanish work is the long and detailed account of the mystical experience which Father Crowe underwent during his last night on earth. This vision is mentioned in the independent account of 1590 attributed to Father Richard Holtby SJ, but only in the account of Yepes/Creswell does there seem to be powerful evidence to accept the supernatural nature of what happened. Of course the Church is cautious and the offical documents of the Cause preserve prudent reservations, but something quite extraordinary happened that night and modern man should not rule out too easily the direct intervention of God in human affairs.

The chronicle of events related by Yepes/Creswell is that when Father Crowe was taken back to prison after his trial, he was not returned to solitary confinement but was placed in a cell with another Catholic prisoner, whose name is not known, but who later escaped to recount what happened. This eye witness relates how Father Crowe told him to go to bed and sleep, 'but I', he said, 'for this one night that remains to me of life, am willing to watch in prayer with Christ, our Saviour'.

The companion went to bed, but could not sleep and remained awake all night watching the priest. He saw him kneel in quiet prayer, but after an hour Father Crowe became 'heated and disturbed'. He went over to his cellmate and finding him awake, said to him, 'Recommend me to the best of your power to our Lord, for I have sore need'. The priest returned to his prayer, but was troubled as before, giving signs of great anguish. 'He continued, as it were in conflict and agony, sometimes speaking low and begging succour from our Lord and the saints; at other times raising his voice as one angry and enraged'. His companion was terrified, but towards dawn, Father Crowe grew more relaxed and began to praise God, and in the morning light was able to explain calmly the frightening events of the night.

Father Crowe said that his quiet prayer of the early hours of the night had been disturbed by the appearance of the Devil, who had tried to persuade him to despair and suicide: 'It will be better for thee at present to put an end to thy life by a knife or halter and not to wait for tomorrow'. The Devil went on to tell him that he would not have the courage next day to face his executioners, and that he would deny his Faith to save his life and thereby condemn himself to the scorn of his fellow Catholics and a lifetime of continual suffering. 'But', said Father Crowe, 'At the time when I found myself in the greatest straits, I saw a great light come in at the door with two persons, who, as I believe were Our Lady and St John the Evangelist, who by their presence gave me unspeakable comfort . . . and one of them said to the Devil, "Begone from hence, thou cursed creature. Thou hast no part in this servant of Christ, who will shed his blood tomorrow for his Lord and will enter into his joy" . . . Immediately the monster disappeared and they likewise, leaving me so full of consolation that I cannot express it'.

This extraordinary experience, which is so well documented, suggests that Father Crowe's claim to heroic sanctity rests as much on his manner of life as on his manner of death, and that even had he not gained the martyr's crown his place among the saints of God would still have been assured.

With a vehemence typical of Father John Mush, the document of 1586 claims that the execution took place at night and uses it as an example to prove the point that it was policy 'to murder us secretly and at unsuspected times (in order to) . . . take us unprovided . . . as also to hinder the people from being present at our deaths'. But no other source makes this point.

The Documents of the Cause accept that Father Crowe was still suffering from the fever that he had contracted in prison and was so weak that he could scarcely walk. His executioners showed him no mercy and beat him to hurry him along. He struggled to climb the ladder to the scaffold and was wounded by a halberd as they prodded him to greater speed. Indeed, he was so faint from sickness and ill-treatment that he fell from the ladder in a swoon, and some of those people present raised a shout, claiming that he had tried to kill himself. But at his next attempt, Alexander Crowe managed to get up the ladder and to hold on long enough for the rope to be fixed round his neck.

Father Alexander Crowe was hanged, drawn and quartered at York on St Andrew's Day, 30 November 1586.

Edmund Sykes

It might seem to the casual observer that the English Martyrs had a most amazing constancy in their resolution to accept death for their Faith, and that with unwavering confidence, steadfast purpose and unchanging determination, they made the decision to surrender their lives and having made that decision never again hesitated for a single moment. If this were true, it could only be by special gift of God or unthinking acquiescence. These martyrs were human with all the strengths and all the weaknesses of human nature, and many of them certainly knew the anguish of uncertainty and had to wrestle with conscience for many long years before reaching that final heroic decision which took them to the scaffold. Edmund Sykes was one who suffered more than most in this way and only after a long and painful struggle with himself did he overcome his hesitations and reach the firm decision which earned the crown of martyrdom.

He was a Yorkshireman, born in Leeds, probably about 1550. He came from a large family. His father, James Sykes, was a prosperous cloth merchant of Kirkgate and was one of the trustees of Leeds Grammar School. In these circumstances, it is likely that the boy received his early education at this school and may have gone on to Oxford University. A document (1595 (?)) in Grene's Collection F refers to Edmund Sykes as a member of Oxford University, but his name does not appear in Foster's lists, which are usually reliable. He arrived at the English College, then at Rheims, on 22 January 1580, when he would be about thirty years of age. His companion for the journey was Richard Hargreaves, a former Leeds merchant who had engaged himself in the service of the College as an assistant to the Procurator, Dr Thomas Bailey, and consequently made frequent secret trips to England on business affairs.

The Douai Diary records the 'return' of Sykes and Hargreaves in 1580, and this would seem to suggest that both had been there before. Probably, Edmund Sykes had first entered the College at an earlier date and had then departed to spend some time in England either because he was sick or because he was uncertain about his vocation. He must have been well advanced in his studies because now, within four months of his return, he was ordained subdeacon, and only nine months later he was ordained priest on 21 February 1581.

Edmund Sykes left Rheims as a priest for the English Mission on 5 June 1581 and returned to his own home district. The document (1595(?)) in Grene's Collection F describes how 'he lived a very strict and strait life, wandering as a poor pilgrim, and coming to Leeds did help many with his holy life and doctrine'. For the next four years he managed to preserve his freedom, but as the same document relates, he then fell sick with 'an extreme ague', and in this condition had the misfortune to be captured by Arthur Webster, the notorious lapsed Catholic now become professional priest catcher.

It was not likely that Arthur Webster would show a sick priest any mercy. He had already condemned his own mother, 'a good and constant Catholic gentlewoman' and his own sister, the saintly Frances Webster, to the horrors of York prison. Now he carried the enfeebled priest to York and presented him before the Council of the North.

Edmund Sykes was committed to the kidcotes or the prisons on Ousebridge, where the damp and cold of the river increased his suffering, and with no medical attention his physical health rapidly worsened. Indeed, such was his weakness that he could no longer resist the persuasions of his captors and he agreed that he would go to the Protestant Church. Almost immediately he regretted this lapse. He was filled with remorse and expressed his repentance. But it was too late; the civil authorities refused to listen any further. His first gesture of conformity was quite enough for them, and they acted upon it. Instead of being sentenced to death as a priest, Edmund Sykes was given the more lenient punishment of perpetual banishment.

On 23 August 1585, together with nine other priests and a subdeacon, he was removed from York to the even worse conditions of the infamous Block Houses at Kingston-upon-Hull. He is named as Edward (sic) Sykes on the receipt of the Keeper, John Beysbeye, for ten priests. (Mr Joseph Hurst, *Blockhouses of Hull*, 1913). Soon afterwards, Edmund Sykes was one of the twenty two priests put on board ship at the port of Hull and transported to Newhaven (Le Havre) in Normandy by Robert Ashburnam and Edward Bell, who received the princely sum of £52 from the Government for their services.

By the time he arrived in Normandy, Father Sykes was in a much better state of health. With his companion priests, he was turned loose to fend for himself. With no money he made his own way as a beggar right across France until he reached the English College at Rheims. The Douai Diary for 1585 records his name as one of the twenty-four banished priests then in residence.

Restored in body but not yet in spirit, Edmund Sykes worried about the state of his soul. His lapse weighed heavily on his conscience and he set out on another long journey to visit Rome in order to do penance for his sins and to seek forgiveness from the Pope himself. Having arrived in the Holy City in April 1586, Edmund Sykes stayed at the Venerable English College for ten days. He received his absolution and spent his time visiting the various holy places. In his uncertainty, he considered the possibility of abandoning his vocation as a secular priest and joining a Religious Order, but while visiting one of the Roman churches he received what he believed was a divine revelation telling him to return to England and continue his missionary work, and that there he would receive the crown of martyrdom. (Anonymous paper, probably 1595, in Grene's Collection F).

It was a more resolute Father Sykes who set out on the long return journey from Rome to Rheims. Now he had overcome all doubts. He had made his decision and was prepared to stand by it. He left Rheims for the English Mission on 16 June and settled himself once more in Leeds to resume his old apostolate and await the martyrdom which he was certain would be his fate.

It is not known how long he was able to continue this work. Within twelve months, possibly within six, the story repeated itself and he was once more arrested. This time he was taken in what is now the Middlesbrough Diocese. He was staying at the house of a kinsman of his near Tanfield or Wath in the Scrope country of Wensleydale. Dom Adrian Morey OSB, in *Catholic Subjects of Queen Elizabeth* (1978), identifies the kinsman as his own brother, and it was this brother who betrayed the priest to the authorities.

So Father Sykes endured his second imprisonment in York, but this time with exemplary fortitude. His health was good and his faith was strong. 'He gave himself to much contemplation and prayer, abstinence and discipline; for Wednesday and Friday he used it sharply with much watchings' (Document, 1595 (?), in Grene's Collection F). Another document (c. 1592) in Grene's Collection E states, 'Mr Sykes, a man of great abstinence and austerity of life, using twice every week discipline, continuing it after his condemnation, when, as he found repugnance in himself against it and acquainting another priest with it, he was told that he should not punish his body anymore, it being then about to be glorified. He used once every day to prostrate himself half an hour on the cold ground, to say besides his breviary, weekly the whole psalter, besides many others his prayers and devotions. . .' And yet he was still not exempt from spiritual problems. Dr Anthony Champney (1587) states that while in prison, Father Sykes experienced a great temptation to lapse into his previous fault and renounce his Faith to save his life. His fellow prisoners heard him disputing with some unknown adversary, whom he rebuked and rejected, and later he told them himself that he had been visited by the Devil who urged him to conform to the Protestant religion.

All records of the trial have been lost, but it is clear from Catholic sources that Edmund Sykes was charged under the Statute of 1585 'against Jesuits, seminary priests and such other like disobedient persons'. The Paris Catalogue of Martyrs (c 1628) and the Chalcedon Catalogue (1628) both testify that he was condemned for entering England as a priest and remaining there.

During the trial, the judge himself taunted the priest with his former lapse and suggested that what he had done once he could do again and ensure his own freedom. But Father Sykes was unmoved. 'It was the infirmity of sickness which caused me to go to your service', he said, 'and not for any liking I had of it, the which I have repented and now detest to do it'. (Document, 1595 (?) in Grene's Collection F). Edmund Sykes was condemned to death as a traitor, 'whereat he rejoiced and thanked God'. He was taken back to prison and kept in solitary confinement under constant surveillance so that no priest could visit him to administer the sacraments, and completely alone he prepared himself for death.

The next day there was a great outburst of anti-Catholic feeling in the city of York. Some sources suggest it was occasioned by the news of the failure of the Babington Plot and the execution of Mary, Queen of Scots, but to accept this reason is to accept that the year was 1587. Father Godfrey Anstruther agrees that it was indeed 1587, but the Documents of the Cause prefer 1588. Certainly, feelings were running very high in the city when Father Sykes was dragged through the streets on his hurdle. He was ridiculed, pelted with mud and very roughly treated, but nothing could disturb his equanimity. The days of weakness were over; with God's grace he had overcome his own weaknesses; now the crown of martyrdom was within his grasp.

Edmund Sykes was hanged, drawn and quartered in York, probably on 23 March, in the year 1588.

Richard Simpson

The Padley Martyrs, Father Nicholas Garlick, Father Robert Ludlam and Father Richard Simpson, are all well known in the Nottingham Diocese, and as a group they have been honoured each year since 1898 by a huge diocesan pilgrimage to the place where two of them were arrested, Padley Hall in Derbyshire, the traditional home of the recusant Fitzherberts and now happily restored to Catholic ownership.

The execution of these three priests at Derby on 24 July 1588 caused a great stir, far and wide, among English Catholics, and they were immediately acclaimed by popular voice as martyrs, a devotion which has persisted through the intervening years. In 1604, within sixteen years of their death, a long epitaph of some 193 lines was printed on a secret press and copies distributed throughout the country. By the late seventeenth or early eighteenth century, a series of verses was published in their honour and a copy is preserved among the Eyre manuscripts at Ushaw College.

The Padley Martyrs are still well known and esteemed in the Nottingham Diocese as English Martyrs, but one of them, Richard Simpson, has a special significance for the Catholics of the Middlesbrough Diocese, because he was born in the small village of Well just four miles south of Bedale in old Richmondshire, and belongs therefore in a special way to this Diocese. The proof of his birth is in the Chalcedon Catalogue of 1628 which states quite explicitly, 'Richard Simpson was born in Well, not far from Ripon, in the county of Yorkshire', and the compiler of this Catalogue, Bishop Richard Smith, second Vicar Apostolic of England, makes quite clear in his preface that he has carefully checked all places of birth and gives a definite place only when he is completely certain. Indeed, while working on this Catalogue this Bishop had at hand the statements of both Father Richard Broughton, his Vicar General for the North, and Father Robert Bagshaw OSB, that Simpson was born in Lancashire, but he deliberately rejected these claims in favour of Well. The official Documents of the Cause (1981) state, 'He (Simpson) seems to have been born at Well in the North Riding of Yorkshire; we have no indication of the date, but from that of his ordination (1577) it cannot have been later than 1553'. More precisely, Aveling states he was born at Well about 1560.

The details of Richard Simpson's early life are difficult to ascertain and there is some confusion. The Parish Registers of Well go back only to 1558 so there is no record of his baptism. Father Henry Garnet SJ (1588) believed him to be a scholar of Gloucester Hall in Oxford University, but his name is missing from the accepted University lists. Father Robert Bagshaw OSB claimed he had formerly been a Protestant minister, but this lone voice is unsupported, and the Douai Diary is silent on a circumstance which it always mentioned for others.

Perhaps there were just too many Simpsons for the chroniclers to distinguish one from another. The Douai Diary records a Richard Simpson, who had endured a long and severe imprisonment in York before crossing the seas to seek ordination. Father Godfrey Anstruther OP (1975) is not sure that this is the same Richard Simpson. Bishop Richard Challoner refers to a Father Richard Simpson who was arrested and banished from England in 1575, but at that time Father Simpson of Well was not even ordained. In such circumstances, it is refreshing to find some uncontroverted facts, and from the Douai Diary it is clear that Richard Simpson of Well arrived at the English College in May 1577, that he was ordained at Brussels the same year, and that he set out as a priest for the English Mission in September 1577.

For the next eleven years Father Simpson worked as a priest, most probably in the Derbyshire area. He was captured at the beginning of January, 1588, and in Grene's Collection F, among the writings collected by Father Henry Garnet SJ, there is a detailed account of this event probably put in writing in the very year it happened. This account describes how, 'Travelling in the

Peak, (Simpson) met with a bad fellow, pretending to be a Catholic, and when he had played his part, he recognised the priest for what he was: so at the next town, he had him arrested, and so he was committed to Derby prison'.

'At the next Assize, he was arraigned and condemned, but yielding then to some conference and to hear a sermon, was reprieved. But shortly after, he repented this fact and did recant his doing openly so that then he was most hardly used until the next Assize'. An understanding of these happenings is developed further in the official Documents of the Cause (1981), where it states, 'Apparently he showed some weakness at this time, during the trial or later, and either consented to attend the Protestant services or gave the authorities some hope that he would do so. His defection however cannot have been complete, for he was merely remanded to the next Assize and not released as no doubt he would have been if he had fully agreed to conform to the Protestant Faith'.

It was while Father Simpson was waiting in Derby prison for his second trial that Father Nicholas Garlick and Father Robert Ludlam were arrested at Padley Hall and all three priests were imprisoned together. If Father Simpson was wavering, he was certainly strengthened and encouraged by the presence and words of his brother priests. Bishop Challenor (1741) gives full credit, under God, to the newcomers and writes,' (Simpson) was reclaimed by Mr Garlick and Mr Ludlam'.

There is no doubt that Father Simpson fully regretted whatever weakness he may have been shown and he spent the rest of his days doing penance with fastings, vigils and the wearing of a hair shirt. At the Summer Assize, the priests were charged together that they had come into England after ordination abroad, and all were found guilty and sentenced to be hanged, drawn and quartered.

The cruel sentence was carried out on 24 July. Each was dragged on a hurdle through the streets of the town to the place of execution where a large crowd had assembled. Father Garlick spoke to the people on behalf of the three condemned men and not all the spectators were hostile. There are some indications that Father Simpson showed a little hesitation or fear when he first reached the scaffold, but when his turn came after Father

Garlick and Father Ludlam, he embraced the ladder and kissed the steps and died bravely. An eye witness account in the Chalcedon Returns states, 'Mr Simpson also died with great constancy, but not with such manifestations of joy and alacrity as the others'. Perhaps appearances were misleading, for when Mr Simpson's body was cut down he was seen to be still wearing his hair shirt as a sign of repentance and determination.

As was customary in such executions, the bodies of the martyrs were subjected to further indignities and were set up for public viewing in several parts of the town. An eye witness reported to Father Richard Broughton that he 'with two other resolute Catholic gentlemen, going in the night, divers miles, well weaponed, took down one of their heads from the top of a house standing on the bridge, the inhabitants being in it, and a quarter from the end of the bridge, the watchman of the town, (as was afterwards confessed) seeing them and giving no resistance. This they buried with as great decency and reverence as they could, and soon after, the rest of the heads and quarters were taken away secretly by others', (Chalcedon Returns 1626).

The famous Epitaph upon the Death of Three Most Blessed Martyrs (1604) refers to Father Simpson as follows:

And what though Simpson seemed to yield
For doubt and dread to die:
He rose again and won the field,
And died most constantly.
His watching, fasting, shirt of hair,
His speech, his death and all
Do record give and witness bear,
He wail'd his former fall . . .

And the conclusion of the Epitaph includes the plaintive prayer:

'Sweet Simpson be my friend'.

Father Richard Simpson, in company with Father Nicholas Garlick and Father Robert Ludlam, was hanged, drawn and quartered at Derby on 24 July, 1588.

Edward Burden

Skinningrove, on the north east coast of Yorkshire, does not feature prominently in the Guide Books to the county, and is not usually regarded as a health resort or place of scenic beauty. Ravaged by the nineteenth century incursions of the iron masters of Teesside, it is only recently with the decline of industry that some of its original charms have been uncovered, and hints abound as to what the township must have been in days gone by.

In sixteenth century England, Skinningrove was used as a base for outlaws and smugglers. Protected by the open sea on the one hand and a wide expanse of moorland on the other, it was safe from sudden attack, and its very isolation produced a small but intense community of friendly people, who knew each other well, guarded each other's privacy and secrets, and suspected all strangers. And so it was in 1586 that Skinningrove was chosen as a suitable place of convalescence for a religious outlaw, Father Edward Burden, a fugitive missionary priest, whose health had broken down and who needed the rest and relaxation of a place of peace and safety as much as he needed the rich recuperative air from sea and moor. One is left however with a lingering suspicion that Father Burden did not arrive in Skinningrove as a stranger. He must have been already well known to at least some of the people, either because he was returning to his place of birth or because he had close blood relatives within the community.

It is unfortunate that there is no firm documentary evidence about his precise place of birth. The Douai Diary says he was born in the Bishoprick of Durham, which is usually restricted to the area north of the river Tees. The Chalcedon Catalogue (1628) supports this view as does Bishop Challoner (1741). But there is a paper in Grene's Collection F, written by an unknown prisoner in York Castle about the year 1595, which states that Edward Burden was born in Cleveland to the south of the Tees. Father Godfrey Anstruther OP (1975) accepts that Burden was born in Cleveland and Father John A Myerscough SJ (1956) suggests that he was connected to the well-known family of Burden of Stockton-on-Tees and that this family had several branches living across the river in Cleveland. So if Skinningrove cannot be proved to be his home at least it was close to home, and close relatives cannot have been far away.

Edward Burden was born probably about 1540, but this date is only calculated from the official records of Corpus Christi College, Oxford, which he entered in August, 1558. His university career is catalogued by Foster and described by Fowler in his *History of Corpus Christi College* (1893). From these sources, it is established that Edward Burden became a probationary Fellow of his College in May 1561 and a full fellow in 1563, and proceeded to M.A. in December, 1566.

During his years in Oxford it is unlikely that Edward Burden was a Catholic. He had arrived at the University in the very year that Queen Mary died, and the oath of Queen Elizabeth's Supremacy in all matters spiritual and temporal was certainly enforced on all taking degrees or holding Fellowships from at least 1564 onwards. Nevertheless, at University, Edward Burden cannot have escaped some of the influence of St Edmund Campion, who was one of his contemporaries, and who is said to have filled Oxford with Campionists, 'young men, who became his pupils, and who were such ardent followers of their master, that they imitated not only his phrases but his gait'. (Rev. James Clayton, 1914. *Lives of English Martyrs*, Burton and Pollen, p. 543).

Nothing further is known about the life of Edward Burden from 1566 until his arrival at the English College in 1583. He may have stayed on at Oxford for some years; it is even possible that he took Orders in the Church of England and had an ecclesiastical living, but no evidence of this has been found. All that is known is that when he crossed the seas to the English College, he was already reconciled to the Church, otherwise that fact would have been recorded in the Douai Diary. This Diary announces

Edward Burden's arrival at Rheims on 24 June 1583, and as he was already over forty years of age and an established academic from Oxford, his course of studies for the priesthood was shortened. He received subdiaconate on the 24 September of the year of his arrival and became a deacon on the following 31 March. Father Anstruther says he spent some time in Rome before ordination, but there seems little time for that since he was ordained to the priesthood at Soissons on 13 June, 1584.

Father Burden did not return to England immediately after his ordination but remained in Rheims for a further two years. It would seem that he was already suffering from the tuberculosis which was to hamper his active ministry. The Douai Diary records his departure for the Mission on 22 May, 1586, and for a short time he worked as a priest in Yorkshire. Father James Clayton claims that he based himself in York but it was alleged at his trial that he had frequented the Ripon area. A document in Grene's Collection E, written about 1589, probably by Father Richard Holtby SJ, describes Father Burden as 'a very meek man, and endowed with wonderful wisdom in dealing with spiritual affliction; especially in hearing confessions and comforting and consoling wounded souls. He was gifted with an admirable prudence. He used to travel on foot, and although he was slight and infirm of body, he so overcame his physical weakness by mental vigour, and so burned with zeal for souls that he seems rather to fly than to walk'. But Father Burden was indeed a very sick man, and soon after his return to England fell into what one contemporary described as an 'extreme weakness', and another as 'consumptio pulmonum', the dreaded tuberculosis.

So Father Burden came to Skinningrove to seek safety, peace and the restoration of his health, and there had the misfortune to fall into the hands of a somewhat belligerent Justice of the Peace, Mr John Constable.

Monsignor Peter Storey, Parish Priest of Skinningrove in 1985, has pointed out that in 1588, 'the actual town consisted of just one house and that a Manor House Farm. It still stands and is today the Post Office and shop with two other dwellings in the north wing. It is cruciform in shape and local lore says it was a monastic edifice. Edward Burden must have been staying in this house: there was nowhere else in Skinningrove'. For his health's sake Father Burden went out walking, and quite by chance on the way met Mr Constable. The encounter is described in a paper written about 1959 by one of the prisoners in York Castle (Grene's Collection F). This account does not say how far the priest had walked from Skinningrove before meeting Mr Constable; nor does it say where Mr Constable's house was situated. It states, '. . . walking on foot near a place or town called Skinningrove, one Mr John Constable meeting him, began to stay him and examined him and so took him, and carrying him to his house searched him, and took all things he found of him from him, yea his money, and then sent him to the Council at York, who committed him to the Castle, where sweetly he served God and was a comfort to all his company'.

Father Burden was kept in prison for a considerable time and one of his fellow prisoners was another seminary priest, Blessed Robert Dalby from Hemingbrough near Howden in the East Riding; and there is an old tradition that when Father Dalby was taken off for trial, Father Burden complained 'Shall I always lie here like a beast, while my brother hastens to his reward. Truly, I am unworthy of such glory as to suffer for Christ'. (Father Richard Holtby SJ, (?) c. 1589, in Grene's Collection E). In the harsh conditions of prison Father Burden's sickness returned, and when at last he was summoned to meet his judges, he had to rise from his sick bed. 'The summons so invigorated him, that dressing himself at once, he hastened thither with as much alacrity as if he were not ill, so that the judges found fault with the gaoler for having said he was sick' (same document).

All records of the Council of the North for this period have been lost, but it is clear from contemporary Catholic sources that Father Burden was charged under the statute of 1585 'against Jesuits, seminary priests and such other like disobedient persons'. He was questioned as to where he had worked as a priest and to name those who had helped him. His reply was straightforward, 'You enquire things of me for no good end and therefore I will not answer'.

He was found guilty of his priesthood and condemned to be hanged, drawn and quartered. The next day, he was dragged on a hurdle from his prison to the place of execution outside the walls of the City. On the way the crowd abused him, and a Mr

Ransdell, probably a Protestant clergyman, tried to argue with him, but his reply was to warn the crowd about 'false wolves who seek your destruction'. On the scaffold he asked permission to speak to the bystanders, but he was shouted down with cries of, 'Despatch him; for he is able to do much hurt'.

No details of Father Burden's final moments are known, but that he suffered bravely and persevered in his Faith until the end is clear from the way in which his contemporaries spoke about him. The community of the English College at Rheims rejoiced at the news of his death, because 'crowned with martyrdom' he had gone to join the saints on the vigil of their special feast day of All Saints; and a fellow priest, Father John Curry SJ, who was in York only a month or two after the martyrdom, wrote on 12 May, 1590, that in shedding his blood Father Burden 'gave illustrious testimony to the Catholic Faith', and left behind 'a holy memory of himself'.

There is some uncertainty about the exact date of this martyr's death. It is variously given as between 29 and 31 October. There is no doubt about the year. The official Documents of the Cause (1981) state that Father Edward Burden was hanged, drawn and quartered at York about 29 November in the year 1588.

William Spenser

William Spenser is specially honoured today in two dioceses; he was born in what is now the Diocese of Leeds and he worked as a priest and died within the present boundaries of the Diocese of Middlesbrough. To the people of both dioceses he is a source of encouragement and inspiration, and is recognised with pride and devotion as a martyr who belongs to both.

It is fortunate that so many of the details of the life, work and death of this heroic missionary priest have been recorded by his close friend, that indefatigable chronicler, Father William Warford SJ, who spent eight years with him at Oxford University and then accompanied him across the seas to the English College at Rheims. Father Warford wrote his account of Father Spenser about the year 1597. The original document is preserved at Stoneyhurst, but a copy is in existence among the papers of Father Christopher Grene's Collection M.

It is established that William Spenser was born at Gisburn, in Craven, in the West Riding of Yorkshire. His date of birth was probably about 1555, and the vagueness of the date makes it impossible to ascertain whether he was baptised a Catholic in the reign of Queen Mary or a Protestant in the reign of Queen Elizabeth. While the boy was still very young, his father and mother conformed, or at least pretended to conform, to the Established Church of Queen Elizabeth. They sent their son to be educated at Cornwall, near Chipping Norton in Oxfordshire, and entrusted him to the care of Mrs Spenser's brother, the Reverend Mr Horn, a clergyman who had been validly ordained in Marian times but who had later taken the oath of the Queen's Supremacy in order to retain his benefice. Enid Dinnis, (in *The Pope's Men*,

C.T.S. 1924) claims that William Spenser was sent to his uncle so that he could be secretly educated as a Catholic, and certainly Mr Horn gave every indication of being a Catholic at heart and maintained a full library of Catholic books.

Nevertheless, despite these suspicions of Catholicism, William Spenser entered Oxford University in 1572, where his formal progress depended on his conformity to the Established Religion. Foster's official register of the University shows that he commenced B.A. on 17 May 1576, became a Fellow of Trinity College in 1579 and proceeded M.A. on 21 April 1580.

These were exciting days at Oxford. The glories of Edmund Campion were still remembered and his name honoured. The impact of his startling conversion to Catholicism was still apparent on University life and reports of his ordination as a priest and entry into the Jesuits provoked ardent discussion. His return to England as a Jesuit missionary priest in 1580 and his Brag to the Privy Council caused comment, debate and admiration. William Spenser was still in residence at Oxford when four hundred copies of Campion's book, the *Ten Reasons*, appeared mysteriously around the University, and he must at least have heard about those students who had slipped away quietly to meet Campion himself at a secret venue a few miles outside the town.

Father Warford's account of these times leaves no doubt that William Spenser was keenly interested in religious matters and that he approached all such controversy from a Catholic point of view. He read as many Catholic books of theology as he could find and became such an ardent champion of Catholic truth that he converted many members of the University to the Church, and then followed this up by teaching them to pray and supplying them with such Catholic books of devotion as the Jesus Psalter and the *Book of Devotions* by Simon Verepaeus. Indeed, Father Warford concludes that Spenser saved more souls at this time of his life than he did afterwards as a priest.

Of course, this work did not go unnoticed in the University, and pressure was brought to bear on both William Warford and William Spenser. Life became so difficult and so dangerous that in 1582 they both left Oxford and set out for the English College at Rheims to offer themselves for the priesthood. Father John A Myerscough SJ (1956) says that Spenser was expelled from the

University because of his Catholic activities, but Enid Dinnis (1924) is of the opinion that he was so upset by the news of the arrest of Edmund Campion on 17 July that he left at once of his own free will.

The Douai Diary reports the arrival of William Spenser at Rheims on 2 November 1582, and also reports the fact of his formal reconciliation to the Catholic Church. He was ordained priest within twelve months on 24 September 1583, and he embarked for the English Mission on 29 August 1584. For the next five years, Father Spenser worked as a priest in Yorkshire, but like most successful priests of his time, he covered his tracks so well that little is now known of his activities. Father William Warford reports that Father Spenser had the happiness of reconciling his father and mother to the Church, and that he did this, in disguise, in an open field near his home at Gisburn. He then visited Oxfordshire to reconcile his uncle, Mr Horn, who renounced his Church of England benefice and retired to live with a Catholic gentleman. On 12 January 1585 Father Spenser received a licence from the Master General of the Dominicans to establish the Confraternity of the Rosary in England.

After this, in Father Warford's words, 'he began more freely and boldly to expose himself to danger and to work more earnestly in order to help souls'. The wretched plight of the Catholic prisoners in York Castle aroused his compassion, and in order to bring them the strength and consolation of the sacraments, Father Spenser made himself a voluntary prisoner. He found his own hiding place within the Castle walls and managed to enter and leave without being noticed by the gaolers.

Father Warford has also left this description of the appearance and character of Father Spenser, 'He was a robust man, squarely built, of medium height; his face was long and freckled, and he had a yellowish beard; his countenance was cheerful and his eyes vivacious'. 'From his youth he had always been studious, and, endowed with a keen and clear mind and a capacity for hard work, he became learned above the average. He recited the Divine Office with piety and was very devout in saying Mass. He was most faithful to his friends and exceedingly charitable in doing good to all'.

Father Warford however presents no information about

Father Spenser's arrest. It took place on Lammas Day, 1 August 1589, and is described in an account written by one of the York prisoners about 1595 and kept in Grene's Collection F. This account describes how on that day Father Spenser was travelling, with a lay companion, Mr Robert Hardesty, along 'Bougat' Lane near Ripon. They were not together but keeping a good distance from each other in order to allay any possible suspicion, but just by chance they happened to meet Sir William Mallory, a local justice of the Peace, and paused a while to engage in casual and polite conversation. Something the priest said aroused the curiosity of Sir William and he arrested both travellers in order to make further enquiries. He took them to his own house, Hutton Park, not far from Ripon but in the North Riding.

Perhaps up to this stage the fugitives were in no real danger. There was no incriminating evidence and J.C.H. Aveling has pointed out (*Northern Catholics* (1966) p. 100) that although Sir William Mallory was officially regarded by the Government as a good Protestant, he was in fact a protector of Catholics. It seems unlikely that he would have proceeded any further with the matter had he not received a quite unexpected visit from the Protestant Archbishop of York, John Piers. Sir William felt obliged in courtesy to present his prisoners to the Archbishop, and among the Archbishop's attendant chaplains was a Mr King who had known Father Spenser at Oxford and now recognised him immediately as a priest.

So William Spenser was taken to York Castle on 5 August and this time he was a real prisoner, not just a visitor. He was put on trial before the Council of the North with Laurence Meares as the presiding judge. All official records of the trial have been lost, but it is clear from Catholic sources that he was charged under the Statute of 1585 'against Jesuits, seminary priests and such other like disobedient persons'. As an act of defiance and legitimate pride, Father Spenser dressed himself as a priest before entering the court room. 'Mr Meares would have had him stripped into his doublet and hose, saying his very dress was able to persuade people in the streets to be of his religion. Notwithstanding, they permitted him to go as he came, sharply rebuking his keeper for permitting him to wear that attire' (Document, unknown author, c.1592, in Grene's Collection E).

The unsatisfactory nature of the trial is well conveyed in another document, of unknown authorship, dated about 1595 in Grene's Collection F. This states, 'Likewise Mr Spenser being condemned and brought in, one Mr Bulmer, a gentleman and the foreman of his jury, came to him and required for God's sake that he would forgive him, for that he had, being foreman of the jury, given verdict against him of death contrary to his conscience. Upon which words he pitied the gentleman and freely forgave him it'. This same document recounts how the Reverend Mr King made several efforts to confer with Father Spenser while he lay in his cell awaiting death. 'I come of good will', he said, 'for old times sake, and if you will confer, I will get you stayed, and then after, I will get you pardon'. But Father Spenser replied, 'I do not need to confer with you, because I do not doubt any part of my Faith or religion'. Nevertheless, Mr King pursued Father Spenser even to the scaffold and the priest spent his last moments shaking his head in vehement disagreement with all the clergyman's proposals, before 'he took his death merrily'.

The full sentence of death by hanging, drawing and quartering was carried out in barbarous fashion on 24 September, 1589. Devout Catholics among the crowd collected together the pieces of the Martyr's body and gave them decent burial in Micklegate, either in the churchyard of Holy Trinity or the churchyard of St Martin's nearby.

Robert Hardesty

Robert Hardesty was the layman arrested in the company of Father William Spenser near Ripon on 1 August 1589, and who was taken with the priest first to Hutton Park in the North Riding and then to York as a prisoner for religion.

He is described by the unknown author of a paper (c.1592) in Grene's Collection E as a young man, and the Chalcedon Catalogue of 1628 establishes that he was born in Yorkshire, but there is no evidence as to his precise place of birth within that county.

In modern parlance, Robert Hardesty acted as 'minder' for the priests, and was so engaged in the service of Father Spenser when the arrest took place. The event is described in the document quoted above, 'Robert Hardesty, apprehended upon the way by Sir William Mallory in Yorkshire, supposed in the company of Mr William Spenser, priest, albeit he was some furlong before him and denied that he know the said Mr Spenser, notwithstanding his horse and cloak were taken away and his arms pinioned and so carried through the city of York.' The same document continues, 'He was there committed to the Castle, where giving himself much to contemplation and prayer, desiring always to be solitary, saying his beads every day twelve times, besides other devotions, he began to feel extraordinary sweetness, and thereby grew into a little vain liking of himself. Admonished by his chamber-fellow to take heed of the illusions of the enemy and not to desire to be singular in anything, he began to grow in some doubt about his well-being, fearing that he had been too easily lead into those sweet motions that he felt, and that they might have proceeded from the enemy, whereupon he desired to be confessed to the same Mr Spenser, being in the same prison, but so separated that he had no other shift or means to speak unto him but through a rift or hole, where he began to make his confession. When he came to the "Mea Culpa", he could go no further but began to howl, lament, roar and cry out so mightily and so loud that he was heard all over the prison, his fellow prisoners laying their hands on him to carry him to bed, he smote out with feet and hands at them and cried out pitifully.

Finally, laid on a bed, the light stopped and chamber dark, those about him fell to their prayers. Within three hours the holy man had his senses and was come to perfect memory again, desiring them still to pray for him, saying that he would never be singular again, but follow the order of the house in all respects: for, said he, the enemy had got such power of me for that time you saw me so senseless that all the parts of my body were so sore that I could not abide without crying out if any of you should so much as lay on me a finger, but that it went to my heart every time you touched me never so lightly, as though a knife had been thrust into my flesh'.

This same incident is described by another unknown author in a paper of about 1595 in Grene's Collection F, and he summarises his detailed account of his personal observations of the phenomenon by writing, 'Robert gave himself to much abstinence, fasting and prayer. The enemy did much assault and trouble him, although he frequented the sacraments'.

Robert Hardesty was brought to trial with Father William Spenser before the Council of the North and was at first charged with harbouring the priest, but he defended himself so well against these accusations that the indictment was changed. It could not be proved that Hardesty was actually in the company of the priest, but his past record of Catholic activity was well known and so Mr Laurence Meares, one of the judges, called for the keeper of the Prison, Mr Anthony Ellis, and his assistant, Mr Thomas Earl, to testify that Hardesty had been responsible for actively helping the Catholic prisoners in York Castle by supplying them with bacon, cheese and venison. 'And so the jurors upon their word for this found him guilty of death, whereupon the man rejoiced and thanked God heartily, praying God to forgive them'. (unknown author, c.1595, in Grene's Collection F).

On his return to prison, Robert Hardesty was humbly accosted by Mr Ellis, who said to him, 'I pray you good Robert, for God's sake forgive me', and weeping bitterly added, 'That which I have done and said was to please the magistrates, and I dare say nothing else when Mr Meares called me to be a witness against you'. Hardesty replied, 'God forgive you, and I do even from my very heart'. (same document).

Robert Hardesty was hanged at York on 24 September, 1589.

John Hogg

In the Parish Registers of St Oswald's Church, Durham, under the heading of 'buryings', there is an entry preserved which reads, '1590, 27th May; Duke, Hill, Hogg, Holiday, seminaries, papists, traitors and rebels to Her Majesty were hanged and quartered at Dryburn for their horrible offences'. This is generally agreed to be the only known instance of a Catholic martyrdom recorded in a Church of England register.

Of these four priests, three were Yorkshiremen, but only for John Hogg is there any further information about his precise place of birth. The Chalcedon Catalogue (1628) states that he was born in Cleveland, and the celebrated Catholic historian, Joseph Gillow (1885) has suggested that he was a member of the renowned recusant family of the Hoggs of Ugthorpe.

John Hogg, of course, is important in his own right and of special importance to us because of his place of birth, but he cannot be treated separately from those close companions with whom he shared his martyrdom. They came together in Rheims; they travelled to England together, were captured together and died together. Their witness was individual but their abiding influence has been as a group.

The Douai Diary announces the arrival from Yorkshire of Richard Holiday on 6 September 1584, and he pursued his studies for the priesthood for almost three years before being joined by his fellow Yorkshiremen, Richard Hill on 15 May 1587 and John Hogg on 15 October 1587. All three were ordained as subdeacons in March, 1589 and as deacons two months later. They received the priesthood at Laon on 23 September 1589 and were ready at once to return to England. Their departure had to be delayed however because disturbing reports were reaching the College about an intensification of the persecution in England. The defeat of the Armada during the previous year had lessened the English fears of a Spanish invasion, but the spirit of relief had encouraged an outburst of anti-Catholic feeling and a determination to rid the country of all Catholic influence, native English as well as Spanish. Conditions for priests were even more dangerous than usual and prudence cautioned delay.

So Father Hogg, Father Hill and Father Holiday were kept waiting in Rheims for a more opportune moment to begin their apostolate, and while they were waiting they were joined by the fourth member of their group: Father Edmund Duke, a native of Kent who had studied at the Venerable English College in Rome and been ordained in the Lateran Basilica on 3 September 1589. For six long months the young priests curbed their impatience in Rheims while their superiors tried to decipher the often conflicting reports reaching them from English. They understood that the civil authorities were on the alert but on the other hand they had secret information about the successful development of the security system devised by Father Richard Holtby SJ and Father John Mush on the north-east coast, and eventually in March 1590 the decision was taken and the priests set out from Rheims on the 22nd of that month.

All should have been well. The plans inspired confidence. The priests would land on the River Tyne and be met by Catholic laymen who would conduct them in safety to the secret Catholic houses where they could rest secure, well-hidden from spies and priest-catchers.

The situation as it was in 1589 has been described by J.C.H. Aveling in *Northern Catholics* (1966, p. 159). According to this account, the usual route used by priests to cross the seas was the sea passage from Middleburg in Flanders to South Shields or Stockton-on-Tees. At South Shields, Mrs Ursula Taylor kept a special house of reception for priests, and a former student of the English College, Mr Laurence Kellam, supplied them with food, clothes and money. Another Catholic gentleman, Mr George Errington, (later to be martyred himself) then took over with his companions to lead the priests in disguise to other safe Catholic houses. Already Father Richard Holtby SJ was developing the next safe house in the line at Thornley near Durham only a few miles to the south of South Shields, and for several years the Hodgson home at Grosmont Priory near Egton on the isolated Yorkshire moors had been established as one of the main centres of the whole Catholic mission.

All this was known in Rheims and was the basis on which the decision was taken for the four priests to set out. Unfortunately later developments were not known in Rheims. The whole system had been destroyed. The first underground railway known to history was in disarray. Two captured priests had betrayed the secret of Mrs Ursula Taylor's house; it stood now empty and deserted. The gentlemen couriers had been forced to flee for their lives. Communications with Rheims had broken down and no friendly Catholic was available to meet the priests on their arrival.

The newcomers were obviously unprepared for this situation. They had no experience of living as priests in England and they made glaring mistakes in elementary security. Having evaded the port officials at South Shields and landed, they realised they were on their own in a hostile land. With no one to advise them and no one to guide them, they determined to move south to the Catholic friends that the three Yorkshiremen must have known about in their own county. But to reach Yorkshire they had to cross the full extent of County Durham where the whole population was on the alert to recognise and capture Catholic priests. One experienced priest, alone, in disguise and familiar with the unfrequented lanes might possibly have preserved his freedom, but four young men, in a group on the open road, had no chance at all.

While resting at Coxhoe near Durham they were recognised and arrested. Father John Curry SJ in his letter to Father Robert Persons SJ of 12 May 1590 (Grene's Collection M) states that they were betrayed by someone who pretended to be a Catholic. They were brought before a local Justice of the Peace and committed to goal in Durham as suspected priests.

When the Protestant Bishop of Durham, Matthew Hutton, was informed of these happings, he thought the matter so important that he immediately despatched a messenger to London to seek instructions from the Privy Council. Within nine days Lord

Burghley, William Cecil, replied, and his letter of 20 April 1590 stated, 'For as much as it appears that they repaired into this realm with intention to seduce her Highness's subjects and to withdraw them from their allegiance, we thought good to pray and require Your Lordship to call unto you some learned in the laws to join with you in the further examining of the said seminary priests, that the causes of their coming hither may be perfectly discovered, and if you shall upon conference had with some skilful in the law of the realm, see cause to give order that they may be indicted and proceeded withal by course of Her Majesty's laws, to the intent they may receive justice according to the quality of their offences and convenient expedition'. (Acts of Privy Council, XIX, London 1899, p. 70).

Certainly the Bishop of Durham carried out his instructions 'with convenient expedition'. The priests were brought to trial at once and appeared at the Durham Assizes. Official Court records have been lost but all sources are clear that they were charged under the statute of 1585 'against Jesuits, seminary priests and such other like disobedient persons'. They were found guilty and condemned to death.

Fathers Richard Hill, John Hogg, Richard Holiday and Edmund Duke were hanged, drawn and quartered at Dryburn on the outskirts of Durham on 27 May 1590. They had been priests for less than nine months and most of their priesthood had been spent waiting in Rheims for their call to the English Mission. They had been in England for less than two months and most of this time they had spent in prison. Perhaps they were never able to celebrate Mass in freedom on English soil. The long apostolate for which they had prepared themselves so bravely was denied them, but their mission was no failure. They came to save souls and they saved them not by persuasive words but by the manner of their deaths on the scaffold. Indeed their deaths made such a profound impression on the people of Durham that many were converted to the Faith, and three months later Father Henry Garnett SJ could express his regret that he did not have enough priests to deal with all the people who wished to return to the Catholic Faith. (Letter to the Jesuit General, 13 September 1590; in Jesuit General Archives 651/624).

The scenes at the execution are described by an eye-witness in a document of about 1592 in Grene's Collection E. 'When these martyrs were offered their pardons if they would go to church, some bystanders said boldly that they would rather die themselves than any of them should relent. Others saying: "They have done their parts. If we be damned it is our own fault. This is preaching to us. They die for Him who died for us". And when their heads were cut off and held up, as the manner is, not one would say, God save the Queen, except the catchpoles (the Sheriff's men) and a minister or two'. The same document quotes the words of the four common criminals who were executed at the same time as the four martyrs, and 'who protested that they would die in the same Faith these priests had died for. "It is for certain", they said, "they were God's priests"'.

The fame of the Martyrs was incorporated into local folk lore. Father Cuthbert Trollop, Vicar General in the North reported in the Chalcedon Returns of 1626 that 'the well out of which they took water to boil the quarters of these four martyrs did presently drie up, and so continued for many years after, as was known and noted by different people in the country'. And 117 years after the event, Father John Laxley affirmed the same belief when he wrote to Father John Knaresborough on 17 July 1707: 'When Mr Holiday, Mr Hogg and Mr Hill were put to death at Durham, a brook near the common gallows, at the time of their execution ceased to flow and has remained so ever since, and is thence called Dryburn to this day . . . This is a constant tradition here'. (Document DDEV/67/2 in Humberside County Record Office, Beverley). But the value of folk lore is limited. It usually encloses a kernel of truth but the details are often imaginary. And so it is with the derivation of the place-name Dryburn. The belief emphasises the impact that the martyrs had on the local people, but unfortunately the name was in use long before their time of execution.

Father Yaxley, in this letter of 1707, relates another old tradition connected with these four martyrs and their influences over the people. He was told by 'the present Mr Thomas Maire of Lartington' that his great grandparents, Mr Robert Maire of Hardwick, County Durham and his wife, formerly Miss Grace Smith of Durham, were both present as Protestants at the execution of the martyrs, but 'being much moved at their courage and constancy, were thereupon converted. The gentlewoman's father, who was very rich and a puritanical man, was so exasperated at this, that he made his last testament, (which is yet kept in the archives of Durham) and gave his remaining substance to the public uses and pretended charities for that city, unless his graceless daughter Grace, as he calls her in his will, should conform, and if so, for every Sunday she went to church, he ordered £100 for her, until the whole was paid'.

Such were the beginnings of the powerful Catholic family of Maire who clung to the Faith for the next three hundred years, giving a Bishop to the Church in William Maire (1704–1769) and several priests and nuns. This Catholic line ended in 1897 with the death at Lartington of Monsignor Thomas Witham, priest of the Middlesbrough Diocese.

Thomas Watkinson

There is no reason to believe that the tiny village of Menthorpe in Howdenshire was ever more important than it is today. Situated in isolation at the end of a country lane, almost marooned on the banks of the Derwent, largely cut off by open fields from any centre of population, its few inhabitants have lived their own quiet country life for centuries, undisturbed, one would expect, by any events taking place in the larger world outside.

And yet, most surprisingly, this little hamlet played a significant role in the great religious upheaval of sixteenth-century England and gave to the Catholic Church no fewer than four martyrs, whose Causes have been officially recognised by the Church: Blessed William Freeman and Blessed Robert Watkinson were seminary priests born in the village and Robert Thorpe, another seminary priest, and Thomas Watkinson, an elderly layman, were arrested in the village for their Catholic activities.

Of course, Menthorpe was in Babthorpe country and the power and influence of that illustrious Catholic family must have had its effect on the religious life of the people, but this can only be a partial explanation of the faith and courage of simple Catholics who braved the world for conscience's sake. The persistence of the faith in Howdenshire in general and Menthorpe in particular remains one of the great unsolved mysteries of our Catholic past, but no search for understanding can belittle in any way the extraordinary fact that in these isolated pockets of the East Riding so many Catholics stood firm in their allegiance while all around them other Catholics hesitated and surrendered to the Protestant might.

Thomas Watkinson was a typical Menthorpe Catholic of his

time. He was no longer a young man. In her Narrations of 1620, Lady Grace Babthorpe refers to him as 'the good, old man', and in his *Annals of Queen Elizabeth* (c.1618) Dr Anthony Champney describes him as 'a timid old man, living a solitary life in his own home'. More information is available from an unidentified Catholic prisoner writing from York Castle about the year 1595 (Grene's Collection F). This document states that Thomas Watkinson was 'a grave and fatherly old man', who had brought up his family as good Catholics, all but one boy who was said to be 'simple and no Catholic', and from this same source it is established that he was a widower and a substantial yeoman, owning land and 'well able to live off his own living'. Another witness, Father John Cecil, is not altogether reliable as a character because his faith was suspect, but there seems no reason to reject the evidence in his letters of September/November 1591 to Father Joseph Creswell SJ Rector of the English College, Rome, that the Watkinson home in Menthorpe was well known to Catholic priests as a place of refuge and that Thomas Watkinson had frequently given shelter to Father Robert Thorpe and even helped him in his priestly ministry.

In 1581, Thomas Watkinson was brought before the Court of High Commission in York and charged with absenting himself from the Church of England services which were prescribed by the law of the land. The act Books for the Commission have an entry for the date of 16 January 1581 confirming the order made to his son-in-law to see that 'Thomas Watkinson of Menthorpe, an aged man' procure a curate from his Parish Church at Hemingbrough 'to say service and minister the communion to him'. In due course, it was further certified to the Court that 'the said Watkinson had repaired to the church and received the communion in his house because he is an infirm person'. Subsequent events showed that this reception of the Anglican communion was a mere outward conformity very common in those days among many good Catholics, and that Thomas Watkinson remained firmly attached to the Catholic Church. In fact, he was charged again with being a Catholic and appeared before the High Commission on 24 April 1587, and probably again on 13 April 1591.

Not all the people of Menthorpe were of Thomas Watkinson's

persuasion. Some openly resented the presence of priests in his house and were on the alert for such evidence as they could lay before the Justices. On the eve of Palm Sunday, 27 March 1591, rumours began circulating in the village that a Mass was about to be celebrated and several villagers determined at once that this was their great opportunity to settle the Roman Catholics once and for all. Lady Grace Babthorpe says that a priest was seen 'by an evil neighbour' to go into Mr Watkinson's house, but she adds, 'or some said that that neighbour of his saw some of Mr Watkinson's servants getting palms, which was sufficient to assure them that he had a priest in his house, for they knew well that priests used to come much to his house, but they could not be sure of the time'. (Narrations, Westminster Archives A VI, p. 367).

Father Richard Holtby SJ reports the same circumstances in these words (Stoneyhurst mss. dated 1594): 'In the year above named, it happened that one Robert Thorpe, a seminary priest, went to visit an old man's house, called Thomas Watkinson, there to administer the sacraments unto him and his Catholic family, and being espied and suspected to be the man he was indeed, was dogged unto his lodgings, and straightaway intelligence was given unto a Justice of the Peace, called Mr Gates, who with all speed (as he was ready enough for such a prey) came with men appointed towards the place, and entering the house, took the foresaid priest with the old man, and carried them as traitors unto York to be further examined'. Lady Babthorpe had no high opinion of Mr Gates and refers to him as 'a man ever ready for such evil employment' and explains that he 'with his company came so early of Palm Sunday in the morning, that, as I heard, they took them in their beds'.

Further details are given by the unidentified prisoner in York Castle (c.1595): 'Early in the morning, came one Mr Gates, who dwelt at Howden and a great Justice in the country. He brought with him a great company, and entering the house found Mr Thorpe and all the church stuff wherewith he meant to serve with that day; and ranging up and down the house, he and his company broke open and took away what they liked.

'After, they went to his neighbour's house, John Freeman, and there finding no such things as they thought, took his bond to appear at the Assizes, which he did, and so was committed to the Castle.

'But Mr Thorpe they carried with them, and Thomas Watkinson and his son, who was simple and no Catholic, and John Hugh, William Parker and Jane Adeame. These were brought to the city before the Council, who committed them to separate places and all fell (conformed to the established Religion) one after another, save Mr Thorpe and Thomas Watkinson, who were both committed to the castle, kept apart, and remained constant even unto death'.

The two prisoners were tried in York towards the end of May, 1591 before the Council of the North. The official records are lost, but from Catholic sources it is quite clear that Watkinson was charged under the Statute of 1585, 'Against Jesuits, seminary priests and such other like disobedient persons' and that his alleged crime was that he had received Father Thorpe into his house and harboured him. The document above mentioned (unidentified prisoner, York Castle, c.1595) gives much detailed information about the trial and imprisonment and it is on this source that the following account is based.

Thomas Watkinson did not deny that he had harboured a priest. He told his judges, 'I received him as the messenger and the servant of God for my soul's sake', and on being condemned, he added 'If I were in place again, I would receive more than I ever did, and now I wish that I had received them more often'. Condemned to death, he was visited in prison by Protestant ministers who urged him to give in and save his own life by conforming to the State Church. His gaoler, Fox, tried to trick him into meeting these visitors, but he said, 'Let them come to me if they be my friends, and come not to trouble me, for now I would be quiet; and if they be ministers, I will not talk to any of them'.

The next day he devoutly assisted at Father Thorpe's Mass and was then taken to the place of execution to die with his priest. Watkinson's sons and daughters greeted him as he approached the gallows and he commended them all to God with his last parental blessing. But when they said, 'Ask forgiveness of the Queen's majesty for receiving that traitor Thorpe into your house', he replied, 'I have not offended Her Majesty in this way. I knew him nor received him for no such traitor, but as a priest sent to do good to his country'. The notorious priest catcher Topcliffe was present among the crowd and made a last effort to convert the martyr, offering him, as Father Richard Holtby SJ relates, 'his life and his lands, if he would become a good subject and go to the church. But he cheerfully refused, choosing rather to be a king in heaven than to live a miserable subject and bond slave to sin in the world'.

Thomas Watkinson, the simple old man of Menthorpe, was hanged at York for his religion on 31 May, 1591.

Robert Thorpe

Father Robert Thorpe was the priest associated with Thomas Watkinson, in whose house at Menthorpe he was captured and with whom he died at York. He was one of the travelling priests of the Howdenshire area at that time but covered his tracks so well that very little is known about his activities. He was known to Lady Grace Babthorpe, but in her old age at Louvain she could only write, 'And for the manner of Mr Thorpe's taking and death, I can remember no more'. Perhaps all that can be said about his apostolate is that for six years he laboured on this mission, and that his success as a missionary is known to God alone. Lady Babthorpe does remember however that Father Thorpe was 'a small insignificant-looking man, shy in disposition and on that account did not attract undue attention'.

Dr Anthony Champney knew Father Thorpe from the days of his youth and described him as a man 'of low stature, of infirm health, of mediocre learning, but of great devotion and piety'. (Annals of Queen Elizabeth, c.1618). He adds that although rather timid by nature and not strong physically, he nevertheless suffered bravely for the Faith when the time came.

Robert Thorpe was a Yorkshireman. The Chalcedon Catalogue of 1628 states this fact, but says nothing about the date or exact place of his birth. J.C.H. Aveling calls him 'a Yorkshire Douai priest, who may possibly have been a native of Holderness'. (*Post Reformation Catholicism in East Yorkshire* (1960), p. 22) The Douai Diary reports his arrival at the English College, Rheims, on 1 May 1584. He received the diaconate within seven months and was ordained priest in Rheims Cathedral on 6 April 1585. A month later, on 9 May, he set out for the English Mission.

Six years of freedom was a great achievement for an English

priest of those days when the life expectancy of the average missionary priest was a matter of months. It is a powerful tribute to the strength of the laity of the East Riding that Father Thorpe was protected for so long. Then came the disaster of Menthorpe and, by 25 March 1591, imprisonment in York Castle.

In prison, awaiting trial, Robert Thorpe was subjected to an unusual experience. He was summoned to London by Richard Topcliffe, the notorious persecutor of the Catholics. So brutal were Topcliffe's methods of interrogation that a new verb 'to topcliffise' was coined in the language of the time, and its meaning was to subject a prisoner to the most intensive questioning while inflicting on him every known method of torture. Topcliffe specialised in the Gestapo techniques of the sixteenth century. It is not known why an insignificant priest like Father Thorpe should have been so specially selected by Richard Topcliffe, but the fact is attested in Father John Cecil's letter of 1st October, 1591 to Father Robert Persons SJ (Catholic Record Society, vol. V, p. 201).

After this torture session, Richard Topcliffe accompanied Father Thorpe back to York and accorded himself the privilege of sitting in with Lord Darcy and the other members of the Council of the North when the priest appeared before them for his trial. Topcliffe was relentless in his pursuit of Father Thorpe but his fanaticism in this particular case is indicative of his cruel determination to ensure the execution of all suspected priests. Of course, the details as to how Father Thorpe was tortured remain secret, but Topcliffe's involvement in his trial attracted much notice and Father Richard Holtby SJ, the senior priest in York, has written an eye-witness account which serves also as a guide to the methods employed in the trials of the numerous priests in whose fate Topcliffe took a special interest. Father Holtby's account of 1594 is attested by Father Christopher Grene, who ascribes it to 'Richard Fetherston, alias North or Ducket, vere Holtby'. It is preserved among the Stoneyhurst manuscripts, Anglia II, no. 12, f59rv.

According to Holtby, Father Thorpe was first questioned by his judges on personal matters: 'When did you first go overseas? Who sent you? To whom were you directed? Where did you go? How long did you stay at Rheims? Who ordained you? What financial help did you receive?' To all these questions Father Thorpe gave straight answers and supplied the tribunal with all the information they sought. Next came the infamous 'Bloody Question': 'What if the Pope should attack the realm in order to establish the papist religion? Whose part would you take?' Father Thorpe answered quite frankly, 'the Pope's', but then added immediately that he would not take up arms but would use his beads for he prayed daily for such success.

Father Holtby's account continues, 'They demanded whether he had not in charge to withdraw the Queen's subjects from their allegiance to their Sovereign. And he answered, "No". They asked where he had exercised his priestly functions in ministering the sacraments etc. He answered flatly that he would not tell them. They asked whether, if he had authority from the Pope to kill the Queen, would he exercise it or not. And he answered that he would not'. The line of questioning and the answers show that Father Thorpe made no attempt to deny his priesthood but at the same time used every endeavour to emphasise his loyalty to Queen and country.

Father Holtby is also able to quote a letter which was written in prison by Father Thorpe but which was intercepted by the authorities and introduced in the trial as evidence. The letter reads, 'This is to inform you that I have, by Divine Grace, overcome all the temptations against those great bulls of Bashan. When I was examined before Meares, Purfrey, Rookeby and Topcliffe upon certain questions, I answered both with the Holy Scriptures and Holy Doctors unto my simple knowledge. But they replied again, "Thy coming from beyond the seas is treason; we trouble thee not for religion but for treason"; in so much that Meares in a flattering manner said, "Thou art a simple man, be a good subject and go to church and hear a sermon, and use what religion thou wilt, and thou shalt be free from all calamities, troubles and torments". '"Lo," said I then, "This is great treason; if I would do as you do, and condemn my sely (defenceless) soul, all should be well".

'After my trial, being found guilty, they asked me what I could say for myself that I should not be condemned for treason. I answered, "I am a Catholic priest, sent by authority of the Catholic Church to persuade the people from their sins and wickedness, and to serve God and do the office of priest. . ." "Treason", say they, "thou must obey the Queen". I said, "Render unto Caesar the things that are Caesar's and to God the things that are God's. For we must obey God and the Church first, and then the Queen in all temporal causes, but not in ecclesiastical causes". And they then interrupted me, saying "That is treason".

'I then answering again said, "You promised me, if I would go to the church and hear a sermon etc. that I should go free". But they denied it. I said, "Mr Meares did persuade me".

'"Lo, good people", said I, "This is great Treason," with a loud voice, for by means of their great clamour, I could not be heard.'

Father Thorpe concludes his letter by addressing the recipient directly, 'Thus taking my leave, I cease to trouble you any longer. I give you adieu and my last farewell in this life, until we shall all meet, by God's grace, in the celestial and joyful place, where everlasting joy and comfort be'.

Back in prison, now awaiting execution, Father Thorpe was subject like his companion Thomas Watkinson to the importunities of the visiting Protestant clergymen, who followed him even to the gallows. And with them, of course, came Richard Topcliffe.

From the scaffold, 'Mr Thorpe stoutly answered the ministers and willed the people to take heed of them, for the taught them a false faith and naughty, heretical doctrine'. (account of an unknown prisoner in York Castle, c.1595, in Grene's Collection F). Father Holtby relates, 'Topcliffe at the execution was so moved with rage at the good man's words, whereby he exhorted men to become Catholic and to beware of such tyrants as he was, that he bid the executioner dispatch his office, or else, he himself would come and do it.'

Father Robert Thorpe was hanged, drawn and quartered at the Knavesmire, York on 31 May, 1591, just a few moments before his friend and protector Thomas Watkinson was hanged. 'He died', said Dr Anthony Champney (c.1618) very simply, 'because he was a priest'.

Joseph Lambton

The occasional failures of a security system are usually better known than the more frequent successes, and the value of Father Richard Holtby's organisation for introducing Catholic priests into north-east England should not be judged by the number of martyrs it produced. The Government pressures of 1590, which resulted in the capture of Father John Hogg and his companions exposed the Catholic system at its weakest, and are but part of the prolonged story of those 'cat and mouse' tactics, in which the 'mouse', sometimes but not always, suffered.

According to Miss Anne M.C. Forster, (*Biographical Studies*, vol. 3, no. 5, p. 325) the secret route via the Tyne had been in use for some time and it is probable that George Errington was working on it as a courier long before his first arrest in 1585. St John Boste knew this route, as did Grateley, the apostate and spy, in 1586. The Government seems to have had the whole operation under observation long before its pretended discovery 'by two priests taken about Dover' in 1589. Information was then passed on by Walsingham to the Dean (later the Bishop) of Durham, Toby Matthew, with instructions to employ Henry Sanderson 'to break up the rest of that traitorous crew'. So pressure was continued for several years to obstruct the best endeavours of the Catholic agents at the ports, while keeping a sharp look out for Catholic priests on every incoming ship. But so many Government spies and watchers and searchers cost money, and a modern historian, M.J. Cashman, has been able to discover from the account books of the city of Newcastle-upon-Tyne much information about the activities of Government agents and the Catholic response. (*Recusant History*, vol. 10, no. 4, p. 231.)

It is Cashman who has established that when Father Joseph Lambton sailed up the Tyne in the early summer of 1592, his arrival was eagerly awaited by both friend and foe. An intercepted letter among the Newcastle accounts gives the information that Mr Kellam had given £14 'to a man in South Shields to make ready a chamber very secretly for two unknown persons', and knowing Mr Kellam's close connections with Ursula Taylor's house of refuge for priests, the authorities had no doubt that the arrival of priests was imminent. A plan was outlined to arrest both priests on arrival, but this seems to have misfired and Cashman suggests that perhaps a friendly Justice of the Peace passed on a warning. On the other hand, an account in the *Annuae Litterae Societatis Jesu* (1593) says that Lambton was arrested as he left the ship but escaped almost immediately. Whatever happened, the priest managed to get away from South Shields in safety and then had the misfortune to be captured in Newcastle-upon-Tyne just a few days later.

Joseph Lambton was still a very young man when he returned to England. His date of birth has been calculated as towards the end of May 1568. He was born in Malton, the second son of Thomas Lambton of Malton and a descendant of the renowned Sir John Lambton who is so closely associated with the well known North country legend of the Lambton Worm. The Chalcedon Catalogue (1628) says Joseph Lambton came 'from the noble family of Lambton' and he was in fact a nephew of the head of the family, Robert Lambton of Lambton.

Joseph Lambton's family had been settled in the Malton area since 1500. At first they had been tenants on farms owned by Malton Priory but later had a farm of their own at Amotherby. If Joseph Lambton was well connected on his father's side, he was also well connected ecclesiastically on his mother's side, for she was a sister of Father George Birkett (or Birkhead), one of the first students at the English College, Rome, and later in 1608 to be appointed the second Archpriest in charge of the whole English Mission.

And yet there is uncertainty surrounding the boy's baptism. There is no reference in the Parish Registers of Malton, which only go back to 1571. A secret Catholic baptism would be expected, especially with a mother from such a strong Catholic family, but J.C.H. Aveling has shown that the family never appear in the lists of recusants presented by law to the civil authorities. Since there is no record at Douai of a dispensation on the grounds of heresy, a tentative conclusion can only be that although the family had conformed they had nevertheless secured the Catholic baptism of their son. Aveling suggests (*Northern Catholics*, p. 189) that he may have been an individual convert, and this would seem to accord with the views of M.J. Cashman (*Recusant History*, vol. 10, no. 4, p. 233) who points out that Father George Birkett was in England 1580–1583 and that it was surely his influence which was responsible for fifteen year old Joseph's decision to become a priest.

The Douai Diary records the entry to the English College of Joseph Lambton on 30 September 1584, and his departure for higher studies in Rome on 18 August 1589. He completed his studies at the Venerable English College and was ordained priest in the Lateran Basilica on Holy Saturday, 28 March 1592, with a special dispensation because he was two months under the canonical age of twenty-four. Dr Anthony Champney (c.1618) states that the young man had not completed his full course of theology, but obtained leave to shorten his studies because of his zeal for souls and his ardent wish to return to England as a priest as soon as possible.

And so this richly endowed young man, full of good will and promise, completed the arduous journey across Europe and across the seas, evaded the traps set for him at South Shields, and made his way to Newcastle-upon-Tyne, where, in his inexperience, he took a walk in broad daylight along a public street, was inevitably recognised as a stranger and a suspect priest, and arrested on the spot. The details of the arrest are given by Father Richard Holtby SJ in a letter of March or April, 1593, probably to Father Henry Garnet SJ then Superior of the English Jesuit Mission. It is preserved in the Stoneyhurst manuscripts (Anglia I, no. 74). Father Holtby describes how Mr Christopher Lewine, the Town Clerk of Newcastle, despite the fact that his own brother was a Marian priest, arrested Father Lambton and took him to Mr Anderson's house for further questioning. Here he was kept for a time with Blessed Edward Waterson, another seminary priest just captured. Both priests were then removed to

Newgate Prison where they were kept under close surveillance in separate cells until the next Assizes.

Father Lambton and Father Waterson were tried together before a most impressive array of judges assembled specially for the purpose. The two Assize Judges, John Clench and Thomas Snagge, were joined by Henry Hastings, Earl of Huntingdon and President of the Council of the North, and also by Toby Matthew, the Dean of Durham. Present also was the Mayor of Newcastle-upon-Tyne accompanied by his 'brethren'. Such a gathering of judges, some present by right and others by dubious invitation, was indicative of the importance of the trial, the concern of the Government and the avid interest of the local people that a member of the honoured house of Lambton should be accused as a traitor.

The actual charge is quoted by Father Holtby, 'that they, being native Englishmen born, and subjects of Her Majesty, departed the realm, and in the parts beyond the seas, or in the seminaries of Rheims or Rome, were there made priests by the authority of the Bishop of Rome; and so being returned and made residence here, not reforming themselves and contrary to a statute of the 27th year of Queen Elizabeth; whereupon they concluded that they were guilty of high treason'.

The course of the trial was predictable. The Queen's Attorney explained the statute of Queen Elizabeth 'against Jesuits, seminary priests and such other like disobedient persons'. Some of the jury asked for a copy of the statute book so 'that they might proceed the more assuredly'. Judge Snagge said that the law was clear enough and they needed no statute book.

The Dean of Durham took it upon himself to question Father Lambton about his religion. The priest answered that he was a Catholic, and the Dean thereupon seized the opportunity to embark on a lengthy discourse on the Protestant doctrines of justification and free will. The jury then gave their verdict and pronounced both prisoners guilty and the Judges sentenced them to death as traitors. They were then offered conference with Anglican theologians in the hope, said one judge, that 'they would learn more from such a conference than they had learned from Bellarmine'. But both prisoners replied that they had no doubts at all about their own religion, and so were sent back to prison with the final admonition of the judge to William Greenwell, the Sheriff, ringing in their ears, 'Look after them carefully, for they be great traitors'.

The execution was arranged to take place in two days time but had to be postponed because so many people wished to be present. In the meantime, the distinguished head of the Lambton family visited his nephew in prison and spoke to him sympathetically. As a result the Lambtons were deprived of all official positions in the county.

The civil authorities and many officials were embarrassed by the disgrace they were inflicting on a highly respected family, and M.J. Cashman has noticed how often the name itself was suppressed in formal documents. He suggests that the Clerk of the Chamber, George Dent, in spite of his Protestant sympathies, 'did not care to record the fact that a Lambton had suffered the shameful penalty of high treason in a part of England where his name was such a great one'. (*Recusant History*, vol. 10, no. 4, p. 233).

Joseph Lambton's last hours on earth have been described graphically by Father Richard Holtby SJ, and it seems most probable that he was among the crowd who watched the priest die. His account states, 'Early in the morning, the Sheriff came into the prison and called for Mr Lambton alone, to carry him to his execution, who, being not yet risen, got up quickly and desired a little time to bestow in prayer, wherein he spent about the space of an hour. Then coming forth, he was laid upon the hurdle and so carried to the place of execution before sunrise. Then taken off the hurdle, he came to the foot of the ladder, and kneeling upon the lowest step, he made the Sign of the Cross upon it and kissed it, and after made his prayer more than a quarter of an hour. Then going up the ladder, he turned his face towards the people and made the Sign of the Cross upon him, and holding his hands joined before his breast offered to speak: but one bade him hold his peace until the Sheriff did bid him. Wherefore, he stood still in the same manner for a quarter of an hour, his eyes shut as though he were in meditation. And in the end, lifting up his eyes and looking aside, he first cast his eyes upon the kettle of water that was in heating, and after upon the butcher's board whereupon he was to be cut, and with a smiling countenance, turned his eyes from them again and closed his eyes as before.

'Then Mr Lambton began to speak, saying that he asked all the world forgiveness, and especially Almighty God, whom he had most offended. "Good people", said he, "They persuade you that we are sent in for invasion or rebellion against our Prince, but I have protested, and now at my death I do protest that I was not sent in for any other cause but only for the safety of souls."

'As touching his religion, he said he was a Catholic, and for his profession he was a priest, and he thanked God that he was called to that estate to die for it. Then desiring all Catholics, our Blessed Lady and all the Saints of Heaven to pray for him that his soul might be saved, the rope being put about his neck, he was turned off the ladder, and being dead as they thought, he was cut down. Yet the hangman was so long in doing after he was cut down that he began to revive and to move both his hands and his legs.'

Father Holtby's account at this point becomes a little less graphic but his words still describe a situation of horror. The inexpert executioner was unable to finish his gruesome task and the dying victim was left in agony until such time as a French surgeon could be procured to complete the bungled butchery and despatch the mangled priest to his heavenly reward.

Bishop Challoner (1741) states that Joseph Lambton 'died in the flower of his age (for he was not yet thirty) and in the sight of his friends and relations'. Father Godfrey Anstruther OP can be more precise. He wrote in 1968, 'Lambton was only twenty-four years and two months old, surely the youngest priest martyr'.

The execution took place on Town Moor, Newcastle-upon-Tyne, in 1592. The exact day is not certain but it was towards the end of July and the official documents of the Cause say about 31 July.

▲ The Knavesmire, York. The stone marks the site of the gallows where so many martyrs were executed.

▼ Menthorpe Hall, one of the only two houses remaining in Menthorpe today.

▲ Osgodby Hall in the early days of this century. The Hall was subsequently badly damaged by fire and restored.

▼ The Commemorative Board in the Church of the Sacred Heart, Howden.

THE HOWDENSHIRE MARTYRS

1572 THOMAS PERCY Wressle
1586 JOHN FINGLEY Barmby
1586 ALEXANDER CROWE Howden
1586 RICHARD LANGLEY Ousethorpe
1589 ROBERT DALBY Hemingbrough
1591 ROBERT THORPE Menthorpe
1591 THOMAS WATKINSON Menthorpe
1595 WILLIAM FREEMAN Menthorpe
1596 WILLIAM KNIGHT Sth Duffield
1597 HENRY ABBOT Howden
1597 WILLIAM ANDLEBY Howdenshire
1602 ROBERT WATKINSON Menthorpe
1616 THOMAS ATKINSON Willitoft
1679 NICHOLAS POSTGATE Everingham

The original house of Skinningrove ▲ where Edward Burden probably stayed before his capture.

▲ The open field at Grosmont. On this site beside the Esk, the missionary headquarters for the north-east of England were situated in what had been Grosmont Priory.

▼ Clifford's Tower, York Castle. The best evidence suggests that Catholics were confined in a series of dilapidated sheds in what is now the car-park area.

▲ Copy of an old print, formerly in the Bar Convent, of Thomas Atkinson hiding from the priest-hunters.

▲ Concelebrated open-air Pontifical Mass at the annual Nicholas Postgate Rally, Ugthorpe, 1986.

▼ Two portraits of Nicholas Postgate (the one on the right is reproduced by permission of Whitby Literary and Philosophical Society).

Anthony Page

Anthony Page was not born in Yorkshire. He was a southerner and an exception to the usual practice that missionary priests should work in their own home districts. Even in Yorkshire he never forgot his origins, as is evident from his constant concern about his friends and relations in the south, and Father Richard Holtby SJ refers to 'his long and dangerous journey taken into the south country purposely to visit and persuade with them to return home again unto their Catholic mother, the Church of Christ'.

The Chalcedon Catalogue (1628) states that Anthony Page was born in Harrow in Middlesex, but no record of his baptism can be found. The Parish Registers of Harrow abound with the name 'Page' but not one is called 'Anthony'. The Registers of Christ Church College, Oxford report the matriculation of an Anthony Page in 1581 but gives his age as eleven at that time. If this age is correct, then this Anthony Page would have been twenty-one in 1591 and too young for ordination without special dispensation.

The entry of Anthony Page into the English College at Rheims is recorded by the Douai Diary for 30 September 1584, and here he was a fellow student of Anthony Champney, who described him later (c.1618) as 'a man of wonderful meekness, modesty and purity, above average in common learning and piety, who for his singular candour of mind and sweetness of behaviour was dear to us all'. Anthony Page spent a long time at the English College in Rheims and devoted more than seven years to his theological studies. This is quite unusual among the missionary priests of that time, many of whom completed their studies in a matter of months. He received minor orders in April, 1585 and the Douai

Diary further reports his ordination to the priesthood on 21 September 1591 and his departure for the north of England on 3 January 1592.

Father Page appears to have spent all his short priestly life in the north country. Very little information is available but the Government was aware of his presence. In 1593, a spy reported that he was one of a number of priests seen resorting to the 'house of John Hodgeson, called Crowmonte (Grosmont) in Blackamore'. (P.R.O. SP 12/245 no. 24) and G.W. Boddy (*Northern Catholic History* no. 19, 1984, p. 3) names the spy as the infamous Thomas Clarke, the apostate priest captured at Upsall Castle, Thirsk, the previous year. The Government was also aware that Anthony Page had been seen in the company of other known priests from the south, as is evident from the letter of Justice Richard Young, dated 26 April 1593, to Sir John Pickering, Lord Keeper of the Great Seal, (Public Record Office SP 12/244 no. 144).

Father Anthony Page was captured in the big drive against the Yorkshire Catholics which began early in 1593 and which Father Richard Holtby SJ has described in such vivid detail. (March or April 1593, Stonyhurst manuscripts Anglia I, no. 74). Father Holtby has written, 'This year, being the year of Our Lord 1593, upon the first of February, at night until the next day at nine of the clock, being Candlemas Day, there was a general search made for Catholics all over Yorkshire, Richmondshire, Cleveland, the Bishopric of Durham and Northumberland, wherein all the Justices of the Peace and others of authority, with such as favoured the heretics faction, together with the ministers themselves did flock together, entering the houses of the Catholics and all such as were suspected to favour their cause, in so great numbers that it is hard to say how many were abroad that night in searching. For there came to some houses above a hundred or seven score persons to search. Yet I could not perceive that it had any great effect, save that a few laymen were taken in sundry places, and one only priest, called Anthony Page, was apprehended in a hiding-place made in the bottom of a hay stack, and myself with my brother John escaped very narrowly'. Perhaps Anthony Page was another example of the vulnerability of the inexperienced missionary priest, for despite the intensity of the sudden drive against Catholics, he was the only priest to be captured while 'veterans' like Father Holtby escaped unscathed. This solitary success of this Government offensive occurred at Heworth Hall, a well known Catholic house on the outskirts of York and the home of the Thwing family, who were later to give to the Church two martyrs, Edward Thwing (1600) and Thomas Thwing (1680).

A second letter of Father Richard Holtby (1594, Stonyhurst manuscripts Anglia II, no. 12) explains the unfortunate event in more detail, and in a marginal note Father Christopher Grene has added the information, 'Father Holtby seems to have been a friend of the martyr'. '. . . Mr Anthony Page, the priest, (was) taken in a gentleman's house within half a mile of York, whose name was William Thwing, his sister Anne Thwing, a Catholic keeping the house and her brother at that time lying in the city. A little hiding-place had been made in a place where the hay was laid, whither the priest was conveyed for avoiding the period of the search, but the entrance thereof not being well stopped, one of the searchers climbing up upon the hay, fell into the place wherein Mr Anthony Page was, and so was taken'. Father Holtby relates that 'whereat great joy was made' and that the Earl of Huntingdon, President of the Council of the North, was highly delighted because he had avaricious eyes on Heworth Hall, 'which stood in a very convenient place and was a pretty building'.

The city of York was searched at once for William Thwing, the owner of the building. He should have been safe. He was a Catholic who had conformed outwardly to the State, and had been away from home when the priest was captured. Nevertheless, in Father Holtby's words, 'he was apprehended, committed, indicted, arraigned, and in great peril to be condemned, though he pleaded both his absence and ignorance of the matter; and certainly he would have been condemned if his sister had not voluntarily and boldly come in before the Judges and jury, and protested her brother's ignorance of the matter, and affirmed constantly withal that it was her own deed, and that she had received and kept the man of God without her brother's consent and knowledge. Upon which evidence, contrary to all men's expectations, the jury acquitted the gentleman and so he was dismissed. His sister was committed to prison in his place, who, remaining constant in her profession, doth still abide in prison, and (as I think) uncondemned'.

The eventual fate of Anne Thwing is not known. It is unlikely that she suffered a martyr's death, for the Elizabethans were loath to execute women, but how many years she languished in the miseries of a York prison and where she died are facts which so far have escaped the historians. As in most reigns of terror, she was one of those who just disappeared.

Meanwhile, Father Anthony Page was a prisoner awaiting trial. 'He behaved himself so well,' wrote Father Holtby, 'that by his innocent and mild conversation he gained the hearts of his very adversaries, who would easily have spared his life if he would have consented to any little show of giving in or conformity'. He was urged to take part in conference 'with any layman in the company . . . as also to dispute or confer with ministers'. Great importance was attached to such conferences for to the civil authorities they implied the beginning of conformity, or, as Father Holtby put it, 'they were taken for a sign of indifference or of no obstinate mind'. But Father Page stood firm, and refused to talk in this way with anyone.

In spite of his sufferings he remained full of joy and smiled so much in his happiness that the prison officers charged him that he was mocking them and laughing them to scorn.

He kept in close touch by letter with his Catholic friends outside the prison, and especially with his brother priests incarcerated in Wisbech Castle. From them he sought advice and would do nothing unless he first perceived 'that it was agreeable unto the judgment of his brethren'. In his many letters to his friends and relations he showed great concern for their welfare. Father Holtby was obviously in close contact and often visited him in prison to effect the despatch of his letters and to offer him spiritual support.

One letter in particular is of special interest for it was the priest's farewell letter to his mother. She was not a Catholic but was informed by her son that he intended to offer his life to God for her conversion and salvation. Father Holtby quotes this loving final letter in full and recounts its history in these words, '. . . since that time I found amongst my papers another of his own hand, written unto his mother, the which I should have sent unto her for a token and his last farewell unto her, but that I had laid it up so surely, that I could not tell where to find it; but now the copy of it, I now sent unto you, desiring that you send a copy of the same unto his mother, for the letter itself was almost perished with the moisture of the place where it was kept that I could not well send it, lest it should cancelled (fall to pieces) in the carriage'.

No official records survive of Father Page's trial at the Lenten Assizes in York in 1593, but the York Assize Register was available to the compilers of both the Paris Catalogue of about 1628 and the Chalcedon Catalogue which is firmly dated for 1628. In both catalogues, Father Page is accepted as a true martyr for the faith.

Father Anthony Page was hanged, drawn and quartered at York on 20 April, 1593.

Edward Osbaldeston

Osbaldeston in the parish of Blackburn in Lancashire is the birthplace of Edward Osbaldeston. His date of birth is not recorded as the Parish registers go back only to 1600, but from the date of his ordination is calculated to be about 1560. He can be identified from the 'Pedigree of Osbaldeston of Osbaldeston' in the Visitation Records of Lancashire for 1613 (edited by F.R. Raines for the Chetham Society, Manchester 1871), and was the son of Thomas Osbaldeston and the great-grandson of Sir Alexander Osbaldeston. On his mother's side he was the great-great-grandson of Thomas Stanley, First Earl of Derby, who reputedly placed the battered crown of England on the brow of King Henry VII after Bosworth Field.

Despite the ancestral power and influence of his family, however, very little is known about the early days of Edward Osbaldeston. Even his arrival at Rheims is not recorded in the Douai Diary, and only a letter from the Rector, Dr William Allen, to Father Alfonso Agazzari SJ, (Catholic Record Society, vol. IX, p. 40) gives the information that in January 1582 he was a student of either logic or grammar at Rheims. His further scholastic career is fully documented in the Douai Diary. He received the diaconate in December 1584. He was ordained priest in Rheims Cathedral on 21 September 1585. And then, most unusually, he stayed on at Rheims for another three and a half years before setting out for England on 29 April 1589.

If success is measured in length of years, Edward Osbaldeston was a most successful missionary priest. He preserved his freedom for over five years and deserves the additional commendation that even today nothing is known about his activities as a priest. His name was mentioned by a Government spy in May 1593 as one of three priests who 'keep in Yorkshire, but in what place I know out'. (Public Record Office, SP 12/245, no. 24). Father Richard Holtby SJ, in a letter of 1 November 1595, probably addressed to Father Henry Garnet (Jesuit Archives, Anglia

37, 27v–29v), describes him as 'a man of much prayer, abstinence and singular pains, framing himself with exceeding charity and great sincerity to all classes of people with whom he conversed, whereby he got the goodwill of all, especially of the poorer sort, refusing no work or extremity to do them good, though otherwise he were a diseased man of body: so that one time, in a deep snow and evil weather, going on foot and upon the night to help a Catholic that had long been without the sacraments, being but hardly entertained, sitting all night without fire or bed or other necessaries, the which he endured without complaining, joyfully, he contracted a sickness that had almost cost him his life.'

Father Osbaldeston had a great desire to become a Jesuit. Before coming to England, he had consulted Father Thomas Darbyshire SJ, the former Dean of St Paul's, who was now working as a Jesuit on the Continent. This contemplation of the Jesuit vocation may be the reason for Father Osbaldeston staying in Rheims for such a long period of time after his ordination. In England, he persisted with the idea and had conversations with Father Holtby who mentioned in his letter of 1595 that 'he lived here in England after a kind of obedience to one of the Society, desiring in everything to be directed by him, with wonderful joy and sincerity'.

A full account of Father Osbaldeston's arrest and imprisonment is preserved in a letter he wrote, probably to a fellow-priest in York Castle. A copy of this letter is in the Westminster Archdiocesan Archives (A IX, p. 219) and there is another copy among the Stonyhurst manuscripts (Anglia II, no. 12, f45.) It is rare indeed to have such detailed information about a martyr written by the martyr himself, but Father Osbaldeston is very careful not to incriminate his fellow Catholics and gives only such information as is already known to the Government. The arrest took place at an inn in Tollerton, a village in the North Riding about ten miles north-west of York. Father Osbaldeston was travelling but makes no reference as to his starting point or destination. He had with him as companion, a layman, Mr Francis Sayer of Worsall, Yarm, and together they sought to give the impression of a merchant and his servant. Their misfortune was to encounter by chance the Government spy and apostate priest,

Thomas Clarke.

Father Osbaldeston has described what happened, 'The manner of my apprehension was thus. Francis Sayer and I came to the inn before Mr Clarke, and we all came before night, and I knew him not fully, for I thought he had been in the south; and at supper I looked earnestly at him, and me thought it should be he, yet I still persuaded myself that he knew me not, and if he should know me, he would do me no harm, which fell out otherwise. God forgive him for it.' The priest was being a little naive and very optimistic in hoping that Clarke would not recognise him, for only six years before they had been together for six months in the close community of the English College at Rheims, where Clarke was a new student and Osbaldeston prominent as an ordained priest awaiting his mission. Clarke must have remembered Osbaldeston from those days better than Osbaldeston remembered Clarke.

The personal narrative continues, 'And so when we should go to bed, he went and called the curate and the constable, and apprehended us and watched us that night, and came with us to York, and stood by, when I was examined before the Council, but said nothing then that I feared'. The morning after the arrest in Tollerton, Clarke took Father Osbaldeston's horse for himself, 'and he rode on him to the town in my company, and kept a full spur with me all the way we were together, until we came to Skelton, and then he and another rode before us, and there took off me a whole suite of church stuff'. There is no further mention of Francis Sayer, who by all accounts was guilty of the crime of harbouring a priest. Perhaps the charge was dropped; perhaps he escaped from prison; perhaps he was just another Catholic who disappeared in Government custody.

As for Father Osbaldeston, he was first examined by the Council of the North and then kept close prisoner in the house of Richard Outlaw in York. From this house he wrote many letters to his friends, but the letter quoted above is of special importance not only for the details it gives about his arrest but also because of the valuable information it gives about the spiritual organisation of the Catholic prisoners in York Castle.

There was among some of the seminary priests of the time a strong attraction towards the religious life. Perhaps the lonely priest on his dangerous mission pined for the spiritual support of a community, and many such priests joined the Jesuits and later the Benedictines. At the same time, Jesuit spirituality influenced the lives of many priests and encouraged them to form their own communities without actually taking the three religious vows. Within the walls of York Castle, Father Osbaldeston leaves us in no doubt, the seminary priests had set up their own type of religious community. It is from the Superior of this community, which may have been Jesuit or may have been only Jesuit influenced, that Father Osbaldeston sought advice and direction. 'As for myself', he wrote, 'I yield me wholly to obedience to you in that blessed society and number in the Castle, and desire in all points to live in discipline and order, and as the common life, and what I have or shall have, it shall be in common. And therefore, I pray you, direct me in all things both for my apparel and diet and everything, and as my brethren have gone before me, so would I follow in the humblest sort'.

Father Richard Holtby SJ has endorsed the Stonyhurst copy of this letter: 'He had a desire to enter into the Society', but it is by no means certain that the community in York Castle was Jesuit. Rather it would seem to have been like the little community of seminary priests established in Beaumaris Castle by the Venerable William Davies and the much larger community of seminary priests formed by Father William Weston SJ in Wisbech Castle. It is intriguing to consider that the first contemplative communities in post-Reformation England may have had their origins in the prisons, where the religious rule of enclosure was enforced by an unsuspecting Government.

Despite his aspirations, however, Father Osbaldeston was not able to join the community in York Castle. From his confinement in Mr Outlaw's house he was taken straight to his trial. An attempt was made to hush up the whole affair. Father Richard Holtby relates, 'he was sent for privately unto the pursuivant's house with one man alone, and so was brought unto the bar, neither were any weapons used or any other show made about him more than ordinary for other prisoners, as it seemed, to the end that the people should not make any rumour or speech of him or of any injury or cruelty used towards him.' (Holtby to Garnet, 1 November 1595. Copy in Stonyhurst archives: Anglia,

37, ff27v).

The official records of the trial have been lost, but from Catholic sources it is clear that Father Osbaldeston was charged under the 1585 statute 'against Jesuits, seminary priests and such other like disobedient persons'. Father Richard Holtby supplied the details in his letter of 1 November, 1595. When called to the bar to plead, Edward Osbaldeston said that 'he was not guilty of any crime they charged him with, but that he was a priest and that he admitted'. The Court was not satisfied with this and insisted that he should plead according to the usual custom. But he maintained his position and added that he would be tried only by God and 'the honourable Bench', because he was concerned about the jury and did not want 'any poor men to be guilty of his blood'. Ralph Rookby, Secretary to the Council of the North could stand no more of this, and delivered himself of the statement, 'Thou art a traitor, and thou showest thyself worthy of death'. Whereupon the trial was abandoned.

Next morning, Father Osbaldeston was besieged by Protestant ministers urging him to conference and conformity, but he refused to listen to them. He still maintained his innocence of any crime and was not prepared to allow the members of the jury to be involved in an unjust condemnation. In such circumstances, by law the trial could not proceed, and it would seem from Father Holtby's account that Father Osbaldeston was condemned to death in his absence, but at least he won his point and the decision was made by the Judges alone and no juryman was burdened with guilt.

Father Holtby's account of the execution appears to be that of an eye-witness, for he notices that Father Osbaldeston was 'drawn among common thieves to execution' and that he spent a long time upon the hurdle. While the thieves were being hanged, the priest prepared himself quietly in prayer 'as it should seem in some deep contemplation of our Saviour's Passion'. And then finally, in Father Holtby's words, 'Being called to the place of execution, he yielded most willingly to embrace their cruelty'.

Father Edward Osbaldeston, according to Dr Champney (c.1618), was the ninth Catholic martyr in England that year. He was hanged, drawn and quartered at York on 16 November 1594.

George Errington

George Errington was the Scarlet Pimpernel of sixteenth century England. They sought him here; they sought him there; but like Baroness Orczy's nonchalant aristocrat he eluded his pursuers to cheat the hangman and secure the safety of those whom a cruel Government wished to kill. For Mr George Errington was a protector of priests and a principal agent for Father Richard Holtby SJ in the organisation of the Catholic security system for the North East Coast.

He was a member of the well-known family of Errington of Errington, but there are so many branches of this important Northumbrian family that his precise position in the family has not been established. (See Ann Forster, *Biographical Studies*, vol. 3, no. 5, p. 322). It is known from the Chalcedon Catalogue (1628) that he was born at Hirst, which is in the parish of Woodhorn in east Northumberland near the modern town of Ashington, and it is estimated from University records that his year of birth was 1554.

In 1572, reputedly at the age of eighteen, George Errington matriculated at the University of Oxford as a member of Trinity College and his university career is chronicled in the University lists of Boase and Clark. He graduated B.A. in 1576 and proceeded M.A. in 1579, but in order to be admitted to these degrees he must have conformed to the Established Church at least to the extent of taking the Oath of the Queen's Supremacy.

At Oxford, he was a contemporary of William Spenser, the future priest-martyr and William Warford, later a Jesuit priest, but at that time neither of them was reconciled to the Catholic Church. Dr Ann Forster believes 'that it seems possible that the ardour which so characterised George Errington during the rest of his life, was first kindled in the intimate discussions of college circles, and afterwards fed by the knowledge that one friend after another was preparing to face poverty and peril and cross the seas in order to become a priest. There is nothing to show that he felt a similar call, or that he was adopting or intended to adopt any particular profession; but the life of a country gentleman, which to all appearances he was leading after his university years, may well have masked what he regarded as his true vocation . . . the lay apostolate, so vital if the priests returning from abroad were to be brought into contact with the people who needed them'. (*Biographical Studies*, vol. 3, no. 5, p. 324).

On leaving University, George Errington returned home to look after an estate at Ellington, which was close enough to be in the same parish of Woodhorn as his birthplace, Hirst. His name is mentioned in 1580 as a landlord there in the Report of the Warden of the Marches to the Privy Council. (Public Record Office, SP 12/205 no. 13) It was probably at about this time that George Errington was formally reconciled to the Catholic Church and entered upon the lay apostolate that was to be his life's work. The Documents for the Cause (p. 1193) describe his activities as 'escorting students from England to the Catholic Colleges on the Continent, carrying letters back and forth, (probably bringing Catholic literature into England), receiving priests on their return to England, sheltering them and arranging for their journeys round the country'.

The secret organisation of Father Richard Holtby SJ has already been described and reference made to George Errington's association with Ursula Taylor and Laurence Kellam at South Shields. In April 1585, a spy, Nicholas Berden, could report that priests were landing at or near Newcastle-upon-Tyne. 'The priests most commonly do come over in French boats that come to Newcastle for coals, which land the said priests either at Newcastle or in some creek near to the same'. They were then conveyed, Berden said, 'farther into the land', to various gentlemen's houses, where they changed their clothes, and were provided with horses for their journey to London or elsewhere'. (Public Record Office SP 12/177 no. 19).

The first evidence that George Errington was known to the

Government as one associated with these activities was his sudden arrest on Tyneside in 1585. He was taken to London and imprisoned in the Tower. In August of that year he was closely questioned by Sir Owen Hopton and Mr Edward Baker, and the official report of these examinations is in the Public Record Office, (SP 12/181, no. 78). From these records it is clear that George Errington had been arrested on the quayside at Sandgate, a little distance down river from Newcastle, and that he had been about to embark on a French ship, which was waiting for him. He had with him a young boy, whose name he refused to disclose but who was bound, presumably, for a continental seminary. He admitted that he had received the boy from his older brother at Neville's Cross near Durham and that together they had ridden to Sandgate. It was, of course against the law of the time for Catholic boys to be sent overseas for educational purposes, and Errington was in further trouble because he was also caught in the attempt to smuggle nine letters out of the Kingdom.

Arrested at the same time as Errington and examined also by Sir Owen Hopton and Mr Edward Barker was Mr Robert Heathfield, a Catholic merchant from Newcastle, who was accused of passing letters to Errington and helping him to convey the boy overseas. Heathfield was not able to stand up to the questioning. He admitted that he had been a Catholic and that he had been involved in helping a priest, (Blessed) Thomas Alfield, martyred at Tyburn the previous month. He claimed that he had only met George Errington on one occasion and then made the damaging admission, 'that he was never made acquainted with any of George Errington's journeys beyond the seas, but only this last'. And on being offered the Queen's forgiveness, 'if he would reform himself and become a new man, as well in his dutiful obedience as in matters of religion, he protested humbly with tears, that if he may now receive favour and be forgiven, he will forever become a new man and resort to church and do all things as a faithful and loving subject'. So he was released.

George Errington, however, refused to bargain with his faith. He proclaimed himself a Catholic, and there was nothing further to be said. He was kept in the Tower for over a year and his name appears regularly in the accounts presented by the Lieutenant for food and lodging. In November 1586 the name of Errington appears on two separate lists of prisoners in the Tower, and to one of these is added the instruction of the Privy Council that 'he was to be conferred with in point of religion'. Finally, on 3 February 1587 it is recorded that he was released on bail of £100. (Public Record Office, SP 12/205, no. 13). So after almost two years in prison, George Errington returned north to continue his work for priests just as if he had never been arrested at all. He rejoined Father Holtby's organisation and specialised as before in escorting priests from Mrs Ursula Taylor's house in South Shields to the safe houses at Thornley and Grosmont and elsewhere.

He was still at this dangerous work during the Government's severe offensive of 1589–90, and although he managed to avoid capture, his reputation and activities were well known. Toby Matthew, the Protestant Bishop of Durham, referred to him by name in a letter to Sir Robert Cecil and described him as 'a lusty, tall man, well-horsed and armed', who guided and conveyed priests, 'to such gentlemen's houses and other places, as they were assigned to'. (Letter of 27 June 1600; Hatfield House, Cecil Papers, 180, ff127rv). From that time onwards, Henry Sanderson was specially commissioned by the Government 'to break the nest of that Popish and traitorous crew', (Toby Matthew's words), and he pursued George Errington with grim determination. Errington went underground, moving in secret from place to place, with Sanderson always hot on his trail. The pursuit lasted until early in 1591, when as Toby Matthew reported, 'after long hunting from place to place to his great labour, cost and peril', Sanderson 'apprehended George Errington, hand to hand, being their chieftain and guide'.

Errington was brought to York and appeared before Topcliffe and the Council of the North on 22 May 1591 and again on 24 May. He was then committed to York Castle, where he appeared to be living a quiet life until 4 December, when he suddenly escaped, taking with him a Welsh priest, Father George Williams, who was one of his charges from Ursula Taylor's house. The escape is described by Father John A. Myerscough SJ (*Martyrs of Durham*, p. 104), in the words of one of Father Christopher Grene's manuscripts: 'The 4th December, in the evening, Sir George Williams, a seminary priest and a Welshman, and Mr George Errington, a northern gentleman, both went away from the Castle, to the great trouble, discredit and disquiet of the Catholic prisoners, who were locked up and deprived of their former liberties'.

George Errington returned once more to his life's work, but there were indications now that the Government regarded his recapture as a pressing priority and he was for a time the most wanted recusant in the North. Members of his family were harassed and as the result of close questioning at least two of them were convicted. The records show that an Errington of Buckley and Elizabeth Errington of Ogle Castle both suffered the penalties of the law at Newcastle in July 1592.

Another Government agent was assigned to the case to help Henry Sanderson whose lack of success was causing disquiet. The new man was a renegade Marian priest, Anthony Atkinson, who reported to his Protestant masters in October 1593, (Public Record Office, SP 12/245 no. 131) that George Errington had been seen among those present at Mr Claxton's house at the Waterhouse, Brancepeth, near Durham, on 12 and 13 July when Mr Metcalfe had said Mass, and again in the same place on 5 August when Mr Boste had said Mass.

On 30 August there was another report that George Errington had been one of a group of Catholics who had stayed the night at Mr Wilfrid Lee's house in Co. Durham, and that a few days later, at least one of that company had been seen among a group of horsemen, where 'every man had a case of pistols'. On such evidence, the Documents of the Cause have suggested (p. 1195) that Errington was accompanying one or other of these priests on their pastoral rounds. Dr Ann Foster, however is of the opinion (*Biographical Studies*, vol. 3, no. 5, p. 328) that Errington's special charge was for Father Anthony Metcalfe, and she adds the information that the real name of this priest was Hebburn, and that although he came from the family at Hardwick Hall near Stockton he was descended from the Metcalfes of Nappa Hall in Wensleydale.

Watched so carefully, it was inevitable that sooner or later Errington would be caught. His third and final arrest took place in early November, 1593, somewhere in County Durham, but details are not known. He was taken to York on 6 November, and according to the document of c.1595 written by an unknown prisoner in the Castle, (Grene's Collection F) he spent the night in the custody of a pursuivant and was then returned next morning to his old familiar surrounds within the walls of York Castle. On 16 November he made his appearance before the Council of the North and was then formally committed to prison.

George Errington spent the whole winter in the cold and damp of a York prison cell, and was then taken to Durham on 16 July 1594. His travelling companions for the journey were two priests, both of whom had been examined and tortured in London. The first was his old friend, Father John Boste, who had been caught at the Waterhouse by Anthony Atkinson on 10 September; the other was Father John Ingram, who had been captured at Berwick on 25 November 1593. All three prisoners were tied to their horses and had their arms pinioned.

At Durham, strangely, George Errington was ignored, and not brought to trial. Father Boste and Father Ingram were joined by a layman, George Swallowell, and together these three were tried and subsequently executed. Today they are honoured as St John Boste, Blessed John Ingram and Blessed George Swallowell. George Errington was taken from Durham to Newcastle and spent ten days in Newgate prison. The City Chamberlain's Account Book gives some idea of his suffering by noting that in addition to the charge of ten shillings for his accommodation, he had to pay twelve pence for the taking off and putting on of the irons on his legs.

This journey to Durham and Newcastle can only be construed as an administrative muddle. The authorities never seemed to have enough firm evidence to bring Errington to trial, and it is a great tribute to his expertise that he should have been so active and so well-known as a protector of priests and yet always one step ahead of those who sought to convict him of his legal crimes.

George Errington was brought back to York Castle and was simply left to live out his days in the harsh conditions of a prison which would inevitably shorten his life. And so he might have remained and died in prison as a Confessor for the Faith had it not been for the cruel trick of a fellow prisoner, a Protestant minister, who announced his conversion to the Catholic Faith and asked the Catholic prisoners to help him find a priest who could reconcile him to the Church. George Errington was one of those who fell for the trap. He helped the man towards a priest, but as soon as the informer had collected sufficient evidence he denounced to the authorities all who had given him assistance.

George Errington was charged before the Council of the North with 'persuading to popery', which by the statute of 1581 was regarded as high treason. He was found guilty and executed, and he who had worked so courageously for priests, was hanged, drawn and quartered, just like a priest, on 29 November 1596, at the Knavesmire, York.

William Knight

One of George Errington's companies in his martyrdom was a young man from Howdenshire, William Knight, only twenty-three years of age but already an experienced recusant who had spent many years in prison for his Faith.

William Knight was known personally to Mrs Elizabeth Ellison, who lived at Cliffe, and it is on her evidence that the Chalcedon Returns of 1626 state, 'William Knight was born at South Duffield in the parish of Hemingbrough in Yorkshire, the son of Leonard Knight, a good wealthy husbandman'. His date of birth is calculated to be about 1573, but there is no record of his baptism as the Parish Registers of Hemingbrough begin only in 1605.

No details are known of his early years, but Lady Grace Babthorpe in her Memoirs of about 1620, (quoted in *Troubles of Our Catholic Forefathers*, Morris, p. 245) has described the state and conditions in which Catholics lived in that district at that time. She wrote, 'For the poor Catholics of our parish of Hemingbrough, the persecution has been greater than I can relate, for no Catholic could keep any goods, no, nor the poor folks keep a cow to give their children milk, but it was taken from them; and of late years, they forced them to pay twelve pence every Sunday. And of such as had not money, they take their goods, and of the poor that had not great goods, they took such things as they found in their houses, as their vessels, of some of their porridge pots, and of others clothes off their beds, and if they had more coats than that on their backs, they took them, and of one that had, with her work in the summer, got a piece of cloth to clothe her children with, they took it from her; and those they could get nothing off, they sent to prison'.

Coming from a wealthy family, William Knight should not have suffered as one of the poor, but in fact the early death of his father left him in great poverty and it was only when he reached the age of twenty-one that he was able to inherit his father's possessions. 'Coming to man's estate', wrote Lady Grace Babthorpe, 'he came to his uncle about some land which was due to him. Whether the uncle had the land in his possession or the writings by which the young man should come to his land, I remember not; but knowing his nephew to be Catholic, took him and sent him to prison, where he remained till he got the crown of martyrdom. If he would have gone to the church, his uncle would not have sent him to prison, but have given him his land'. (*Troubles of Our Catholic Forefathers*, Morris, p. 245). The Act Books of the Court of High Commission at York show that this was not the first time that William Knight had been in trouble for his religion. He had been accused of recusancy on 11 May 1591, when he was about eighteen years of age, and ordered to appear before the Court with Robert Archer of Howden, Richard Mawtus of Ripon, Henry Green and his wife Anne of Breighton, and Richard Walls, another member of the Green family. Only Robert Archer appeared in court, and he said that he could not be moved to go to church 'nor would not', and was accordingly committed to the custody of the Sheriff. The others could not be traced and escaped arrest.

But by 1593 William Knight was in prison for his faith, and seems to have spent the rest of his life more in prison than outside. The horrors of the Elizabethan prisons have been well described by many of the Catholic prisoners, and frequently prisoners died from cramped, unhealthy conditions. On the other hand, as J.C.H. Aveling has pointed out (*Catholic Recusancy in York*, p. 55), there was no uniformity in prison conditions and in York at least security was often lax and money could buy anything. The Courts were over-worked, the prisons crowded, and from 1574 the authorities began to borrow private houses as temporary goals. Prisoners were expected to pay for their own food and accommodation and it became a lucrative profession for the less scrupulous to undertake the custody of prisoners for the sole reason of making money out of them.

When arrested in 1593, William Knight must have been regarded as a wealthy man, because he was first put in the most expensive accommodation in the palace or the King's Manor, which was the seat of the Council of the North and under the personal supervision of Colyer, the pursuivant. By 5 October, however, it was realised that William Knight had insufficient money and he was removed to the criminal's section of the Castle. In giving these facts, the unknown York prisoner of c.1595 (Grene's Collection F) adds that after five days among the felons, Knight 'came up amongst the other Catholic prisoners'. The Catholic prisoners lived together within the Castle and made the most of such opportunities as presented themselves. They were supposed to be kept apart from each other but the rule was seldom enforced. In an effort to overcome the corruption of the goalers, the authorities had laid down the scale of the fees to be paid. Aveling has concluded that 'three month stay in the Castle would cost a recusant esquire some £16, exclusive of tips and bribes and the fees of pursuivants and attornies'. (*Catholic Recusancy in York*, p. 63).

The Castle was not the secure citadel it appeared to be. The walls were in bad repair and not very high, and Aveling states that the prisoners were kept 'in a complex of patched-up medieval buildings' within the walls. He describes the conditions in this way, 'The prisoners were housed in a higgledy-piggley fashion through a maze of rooms and lean-to erections, often of flimsy materials. It was relatively easy for a determined man to escape by night, and for recusants to conceal Mass-kit and Catholic books. Indeed the recusant memoirs say plainly that many more prisoners would have escaped, had they not been restrained by thoughts of the difficulties they would impose on their families and on the prisoners who remained. Moreover there were subtle reasons for staying. Some recusant gentry found that they could actually save money by being in gaol; and the more pious, in spite of the regulations, found religious facilities in the Castle (the sacraments, perhaps Mass, instruction from priests, even instruction for their children) easier than in the country. At least fifty Marian and seminary priests were goaled here between 1578 and 1603' (*Catholic Recusancy in York*, pp. 63–4).

William Knight soon discovered residence in this Catholic gentleman's club was a hazardous affair. For some reason, perhaps overcrowding, perhaps inability to pay, he was transferred to the notorious hell-hole of the Block Houses at Hull. The Acts of the High Commission for 8 January 1594 record his removal to the custody of John Bestby and John Johnson, keepers of the recusants within the Castle at Kingston upon Hull, but give no reasons for the move. How long he stayed in Hull is not known; very little information is available about any of the prisoners in the Block Houses; but by 1596, he was once more in York Castle. Here, he settled down to the indefinite, relaxed life style of the Catholic community, meeting with his friends and practicing his religion. Strengthened in his faith, he might have endured this not altogether unpleasant life for many years, had he not fallen into the same trap as George Errington.

William Knight was one of the Catholic prisoners who was tricked by the duplicity of the Protestant minister. Dr Champney (c.1618) says this clergyman was a Calvinist; Lady Babthorpe calls him just a minister. Guilty of some misdemeanour, (one source says suspected of bigamy) he was in the Castle awaiting trial and made up his mind to ingratiate himself with the authorities, civil and ecclesiastical, by producing evidence to convict the Catholics. Bishop Richard Challoner, (1741) used Lady Babthorpe's evidence to state, 'This unhappy man, to reinstate himself in the favour of his superiors, took a method that will be justly detested by all honest men of what persuasion soever; which was to insinuate himself into the good opinion of the Catholic prisoners by pretending a deep sense of repentance for his former life and a great desire of embracing the Catholic truth'. (*Memoirs of Missionary Priests*, p. 353).

The Catholic prisoners were not easily fooled; all were experienced in the cautious acceptance of new-found friends; but the clergyman overcame all their suspicions and was accepted as genuine. It was agreed that they should direct him to a priest for his formal reconciliation. Again, it is typical of conditions in York Castle at that time that it should be possible to arrange for one of the prisoners to take a short break from his confinement and enjoy a few days freedom. This is what happened, and the clergyman was directed to visit Howden and seek out Mr Henry Abbot, who knew where all the priests were and who was called by Lady Babthorpe 'a Catholic but newly made so, but very zealous to do good'.

On the recommendation of his friends among the York Catholic prisoners, Mr Abbot accepted the sincerity of the prospective convert and did his best to find a priest for him. He conducted him from Howden to the Stapleton House at Carlton where a priest was in residence. Mr Stapleton, however was adamant that his priest should not be seen in what, he considered, such suspicious circumstances, and so the minister never actually found a priest.

Now at last he emerged in his true colours and made a full report to the authorities. 'Now for Mr Stapleton', says Lady Babthorpe, 'both he and his wife were in great trouble for it, but how they escaped I remember not'. The other Catholics involved were not so fortunate; they could not escape, and seven were charged before the Council of the North. They were George Errington, William Knight, William Gibson, Edward Fulthrop, Henry Abbot and two women prisoners from York, Mrs Ann Tesh, and Mrs Bridget Maskew. The charge was high treason, in that contrary to the statute of 1581 they had 'persuaded' the minister to be reconciled to the Catholic Church. The official records of the trial have been lost but the charge is clear from other contemporary sources.

Dr Anthony Champney (*Annales Elizabethae Reginae*, c.1618, in Westminster archives, FL, p. 937) maintains that all the prisoners pleaded their innocence of the charge. They admitted that they had explained the Catholic religion to him in prison and exhorted him to amend his life, but in no other way did they attempt to persuade him to become a Catholic, and they had certainly never suggested that he should withdraw his allegiance from the Queen. Despite their pleas, all were found guilty by the jury and sentenced to death: the men to be hanged, drawn and quartered, the women to be burnt.

The execution of women was always a problem and an embarrassment to the Elizabethan authorities. Under the common law, women condemned for treason were put to death by burning, this being considered more decent than hanging and exposure on a gibbet. In practice the condemned person was strangled before being burnt. In the case of Mrs Ann Tesh and Mrs Bridget Maskew, the Council of the North sought to evade their responsibilities by referring the matter to the Privy Council, and were duly instructed by letter of 5 May 1597 (Acts of the Privy Council, XXVII, p. 91), that Her Majesty's pleasure was for the execution of the two women to be delayed until further instructions were given. This was tantamount to a sentence of life imprisonment, and they languished in prison for another seven years until what Lady Babthorpe called 'The King's coming' when on the accession of King James I, their friends arranged for their release.

As for the men, the execution of Henry Abbot and Edward Fulthrop was delayed until 4 July 1597. The reason for the delay is not known, but both were hanged, drawn and quartered and are honoured today as Blessed Henry Abbot and Blessed Edward Fulthrop. William Knight, in company with George Errington and William Gibson was hanged, drawn and quartered at the Knavesmire, York on 29 November, 1596.

William Gibson

In her great wisdom, Queen Elizabeth was aware that to destroy the Catholic Church in England she had first to prevent the celebration of Mass and that the way to ensure that her Catholic subjects were deprived of their Mass was to remove the priests. 'No priest; no Mass' is an old Catholic understanding, but the Tudor Queen used it for her own purposes and her persecution became a concentrated endeavour to put the Catholic priest out of action by conversion, banishment, imprisonment or death.

The full fury of the Law was directed against the priest to such an extent that it became inevitable that the vast majority of the English martyrs would be from the ranks of the Massing priests. Of course, there were many martyrs also who were not priests, but these lay martyrs were always fewer in numbers and less well known than the priests. This predominance of the names of priests in all the official lists of Martyrs does not imply that the laity were any less resolute. The Penal Laws were framed in such a way that the usual penalty for lay Catholics was imprisonment rather than death, and it would seem a reasonable statement that more lay Catholics died for their Faith in prison than on the scaffold. The role of the laity was to stand firm in their ordinary lives to protect the priests, preserve the Mass and keep the Faith. It was often an unspectacular role; but behind every Martyr was a devout Catholic community, ready, even as the Martyr was ready, to accept whatever fate a cruel Government should impose; and if that meant death, then so be it.

It is unfortunate that so little is known today about these valiant lay Catholics, and much historical work remains to be done especially concerning those brave men who attached themselves to a priest to share his dangers and guide him through a hostile country. Secrecy was of course of paramount importance and the names of such men are seldom recorded in Catholic writings. Nor is much information available about those courageous Catholic women who kept the Catholic family together while their husbands masqueraded as Church Papists to avoid the Law and provide their families with the necessities of life. The prisons were full of Catholic laymen, and Catholic laywomen too. Many of them died the secret death of unknown martyrs; others appeared on the scaffold usually as the companion of the priest they had befriended. Not many of their names are known, and when their names are known even less is known about their lives than is known about the lives of the priests. For the layperson there can be no seminary records and contemporary Catholic chroniclers tended to write more about Priest Martyrs than Lay Martyrs.

A typical example of one of these lay martyrs is William Gibson. He was a companion of George Errington and William Knight in York prison and like them was duped by the bogus convert. He was tried and found guilty of 'persuading to Popery', and was hanged, drawn and quartered for this alleged crime.

In these few facts lie the true glory of a martyr of the Church, but Catholic devotion yearns for a little more information. What sort of a man was he? How did he live? Where was he from? What did he do? Why was he arrested? It is tantalising to know so much and yet so little about a man who may one day be recognised by the Church as a Saint of God. Sadly, very little can be added. He was known to Mrs Elizabeth Ellison, who is recorded in Peacock's *List of Roman Catholics in the County of Yorkshire* as widow of John Ellison. In 1604, she was living in the village of Cliffe near Hemingbrough, and this might suggest that William Gibson was connected with the East Riding. Mrs Ellison's statement is in the Chalcedon Returns of 1626: 'William Gibson, born (as is thought) about Ripon, was many years a prisoner in York Castle for his religion, a man of extraordinary virtue and example. He was condemned for persuading felons'.

The Act Books of the Court of High Commission at York provide the only known official reference to Gibson. They state 'that on 27th February, 1581, was brought before the said Commissioners, Elizabeth Thynne, gentlewoman and William Gibson, her servant, and being called by the said Commissioners concerning their going to church to hear divine service and sermons, they both refused to enter bonds to that end; and thereupon were committed prisoners to the Castle at York'. As William Gibson was said by Mrs Ellison to have spent many years as a prisoner in York Castle, it is possible that he remained there from his conviction for fifteen years until his death in 1596. J.C.H. Aveling (*Northern Catholics*, p. 187), has established that Mrs Elizabeth Thynne lived at Brafferton in the old wapentake of Bulmer, a few miles north of York, and this would be where William Gibson lived and worked at least for a time.

A few facts and a few conjectures make up the life story of William Gibson, but nothing can diminish the splendour of his hidden Catholic life which enabled him to accept Martydom so readily on 29 November, 1596.

Peter Snow

According to Father Ralph Fisher's statement in the Chalcedon Returns of 1626, Peter Snow was 'born in Ripon or thereabouts', and as Ripon is undoubtedly in the West Riding, this martyr is commonly regarded as belonging more to the present diocese of Leeds than to Middlesbrough. But the claims of the Middlesbrough Diocese should not be overlooked. If Peter Snow was born not in Ripon but 'thereabouts', then it should be remembered that much of the area around Ripon is north and east of the adjacent River Ure and therefore part of Richmondshire and the North Riding.

Precise information is lacking, and there are four references in the Second Douai Diary to Father Peter Snow as being from the Diocese of York. These strengthen the case for Ripon as his birthplace. But there is also a very significant entry in the First Douai Diary (p. 115) to the effect that Peter Snow was of the Diocese of Chester. This has been dismissed too lightly as 'evidently an error' by the Documents for the Cause. In fact, it has a special significance. Local Catholic historians are well aware that the powerful archdeaconry of Richmondshire was removed from the diocese of York in 1541 to form part of the new diocese of Chester, and that in seeking the birth places of recusants the description 'from Yorkshire and from the Diocese of Chester' is sufficient evidence to establish that this person was born in Richmondshire. It is not unreasonable then to make some claim that Peter Snow (of Yorkshire and the diocese of Chester) should be honoured as one of the Richmondshire martyrs.

Of his early life very little information is available. The best that can be said is that he must have been born before 1574.

Nothing is known of his family or early education. His arrival at the English College, Rheims is recorded in the Douai Diary for 17 April 1589. He was ordained to the priesthood at Soissons on 31 March 1591 and left for the English Mission on 15 May 1591. For the next seven years he worked as a priest. The Documents of the Cause state that 'he seems to have worked entirely in his native Yorkshire'. Father John Myerscough SJ (*Martyrs of Durham*, p. 115) is a little more precise and claims, 'he laboured in the East and North Ridings'.

Peter Snow was a typical missionary priest of his time, covering his tracks so well that even today his movements cannot be traced. He was sighted once at Grosmont on the North Yorkshire moors, and the apostate priest Thomas Clarke includes his name as one of the priests he had seen at Mr John Hodgson's house there, but he gives no date and no further details. (Public Record Office, SP 12/245). Even the details of his capture are scanty. Father Ralph Fisher in the Chalcedon Reports of 1626 gives the information that Father Peter Snow was captured in company with his guide and protector, Mr Ralph Grimston of Nidd Hall, near Knaresborough on 1 May 1598, while both 'were going towards York'. He adds only one detail: that the layman was in special trouble with the authorities for trying to prevent the arrest of the priest' by lifting up his weapon in the defence of him'.

This Mr Ralph Grimston is often confused with the Mr Thomas Grimston who was gaoled in 1581 for harbouring St Edmund Campion during his missionary visit to Allertonshire, but J.C.H. Aveling has clearly demonstrated that Thomas Grimston of Grimston Garth in the East Riding and Birkby on the River Wiske near Northallerton had conformed to the established Church by 1583, (*Northern Catholics*, p. 117) and had wavered earlier when questioned about Campion's visit. Ralph Grimston was made of sterner stuff. He was no doubt a relative of Thomas Grimston (and thus a relative also of Cardinal William Allen) but he remained always a firm Catholic sending his sons overseas to school, supporting an exiled schoolmaster in Paris, paying his fines and enduring York prison 1593–4, while his home at Nidd Hall was constantly at the disposal of the missionary priests.

Father Peter Snow and Mr Ralph Grimston were charged together before the Council of the North most probably in early June. The official records of the trial are no longer in existence, but from Catholic sources it is clear that they were charged under the Statute of Queen Elizabeth of 1585 'against Jesuits, seminary priests and such other like disobedient persons'. Dr Anthony Champney (*Annales Elizabethae Reginae*, c.1618) states categorically that Peter Snow was condemned to death because he was a priest, ordained overseas, who had returned to England, and that Ralph Grimston was condemned for harbouring him.

The executions took place at the Knavesmire, York on 15 June 1598. Father Peter Snow was hanged, drawn and quartered; Mr Ralph Grimston was hanged.

Edward Thwing

The ruins of Kilton Castle, set on a rocky spur in a valley not far from Brotton in North Yorkshire, are a poignant reminder of the power and influence of the ancient family of Thwing. Seven hundred years ago, Sir Robert Thwing, lord of Kilton, was a local Robin Hood, robbing the rich to help the poor. Another member of the same family was the Augustinian Prior, John de Thweng, who was canonised by Pope Boniface IX in 1401 and is honoured today as St John of Bridlington.

In the 1560's, the Thwings of Kilton acquired the manor of Heworth, York, when the head of the family, Thomas Thwing, a very successful lawyer, married the heiress, Elizabeth Kellet. Edward Thwing, according to J.C.H. Aveling, was the son of this marriage (*Catholic Recusancy in York*, p. 23). He was also, it would seem, the brother of that heroic lady, Anne Thwing, who saved the life of her other brother, William, in 1593 by confessing that she was responsible for harbouring the priest, Father Anthony Page.

Despite the fact that his father and mother never appeared to be recusants, Edward Thwing was fully a Catholic when he arrived at the English College at Rheims on 22 July 1583. At least the Douai Diary makes no reference to the need for any form of reconciliation when it reports his arrival in the party of ten new students conducted to the College by the future martyr, Blessed Edward Stransham.

When he began his studies for the priesthood, Edward Thwing was only eighteen years of age and suffering from ill-health. Within three weeks of his arrival at Rheims, he was sent away to some unknown destination possibly for a year's study in a more congenial climate. He returned in the summer of the following year, but was then sent almost immediately on 24 September 1584 to Pont-à-Mousson, no doubt to the Jesuit College there. He was back in Rheims on 20 July 1585, and continued his studies uninterrupted for the next two years. In November 1587 he was sent to the English College, Rome, but after three years there his health once more gave cause for anxiety and he returned to Rheims in 1590. He was ordained priest at Laon on 20 December 1590. and his Superiors decided that he was not strong enough for the English Mission and appointed him to the Seminary staff. For the next seven years he taught logic and later Greek and Hebrew to the students. Dr Anthony Champney, who was one of Father Thwing's pupils, described him as a man of wonderful meekness, piety and mortification, and stressed the great patience he showed in his many illnesses, especially when suffering from a painful ulcer on the knee.

In 1592 Father Thwing was sent to a spa in the Low Countries to take the thermal waters in an attempt to regain his health, and this treatment might have been successful. The English College moved back to Douai from Rheims in 1593 and one of the incidental consequences was a neglect of the Diary. Edward Thwing is not mentioned again until 1597, when his departure for the English Mission is recorded. Father Godfrey Anstruther OP suggests that 'he left for England apparently in bad health', (*Seminary Priests*, vol. 1, p. 356) and Dr Anthony Champney has expressed the contemporary opinion that one of the major reasons for sending him back to England was the hope that he would benefit from his native air.

Whatever the state of his health might have been, Father Thwing was able to work as a priest in England for three years. He does not seem to have returned to his native Yorkshire but settled in Lancashire. In 1598 he was one of the priests who signed the letter to Pope Clement VIII in support of the Archpriest, Father George Blackwell. In Lancashire, he joined up with Father Robert Nutter OP, who had just escaped from Wisbech Castle after sixteen years imprisonment. Together, the two priests were returning from a visit to Father Richard Cowling, another native of York, when they were recognised and arrested. As a prisoner in Lancaster Castle, Edward Thwing was interrogated by Richard Vaughan, Bishop of Chester and Mr Thomas Hesketh, Attorney to the Court of Wards, and the latter reported on 17 August 1600 to Sir Robert Cecil, Her Majesty's Secretary of State, (Cecil Papers, 87, f107): 'The true name of the other priest was Edward Thwing, born in the city of York. He had named himself Hylton. He was sometimes called Nysaunce. The Bishop and I did examine him. It appeared that he had been a scholar of some understanding and much esteemed among the papists. And yet he did defend among many other gross opinions that without offence he might equivocate (as he termed it) before the magistrate, which equivocation is plain lying, for being blamed because he had affirmed upon his first examination that he was born in Northumberland, whereas it appeared that he was born in the city of York, he said he did equivocate'.

On 4 July 1600, a public disputation was arranged in Lancaster Castle, and a large crowd attended. Father Nutter and Father Thwing were confronted by the Protestant Vicars of Lancaster and Kendal. Father Thwing and the Vicar of Kendal seem to have done most of the talking. 'The other two very rarely meddled', wrote Father John Knaresborough (*Foul Draughts*, c.1720, Humberside County Record Office, DDEV/67/2). In prison, Father Thwing busied himself writing many letters to his brother, his sister and his friends. Dr Thomas Worthington, the President of Douai has preserved two of these letters which he himself received. (*A Relation of Sixteen Martyrs*, Douai, 1601, pp. 91–94).

In the first letter, Father Thwing wrote, 'Myself am now a prisoner for Christ in Lancaster Castle, expecting nothing but execution at the next Assizes. I desire you commend me to the devout prayers of my friends with you, that by their help, I may consummate my course to God's glory and the good of my country. I pray God prosper you and all yours for ever. From my prison and paradise, this last day of May, 1600, E.Th.'. In the second letter he wrote, 'This day the judges come to Lancaster, where I am in expectation of a happy death, if it so please God Almighty. I pray you commend me most dearly to my uncle and my brother. I pray God bless them both and to all the good priests and scholars, whose good endeavours prosper, to His own more Glory . . . Before this comes unto you, I shall, if God make me worthy, conclude an unhappy life with a most happy death . . . From Lancaster Castle, the 21st of July, this holy year of 1600. All yours in Christ, Edward Thwing'.

Nutter and Thwing were tried at the Summer Assizes at Lancaster in July, 1600. All official records of the trial have been lost, but it is clear from contemporary Catholic sources that they were tried under the statute of Queen Elizabeth, 1585, 'against Jesuits, seminary priests and such other like disobedient persons'. Both were found guilty and sentenced to be hanged, drawn and quartered.

In his letter to Sir Robert Cecil of 17 August 1600 (previously quoted) Mr Thomas Hesketh reported, 'At the execution of this priest, (Father Thwing), he was demanded by me the like questions as were proposed to the friar. He acknowledged Her Majesty to be his lawful Queen and that he would pray for her. But being urged further whether she ought to be so, the Pope's excommunication notwithstanding, and whether he would affirm so much if the Pope had not allowed certain faculties to him and others for that purpose: to the first he did bid us look to it ourselves, and to the second he would not answer. And thereupon was executed without delay'.

Mr Hesketh goes on to comment, 'Many that were favourers of popery and were present at the arraignment and execution, (as I hear) did say that they would not have thought that priests held such gross opinions against Her Majesty or in religion', and he adds, 'I do not doubt but much good will come by this little severity as well to terrify the priests from these parts as for the satisfaction of the people'. But Mr Hesketh's impression is not supported by contemporary Catholic accounts. Father Richard Cowling SJ who had left England soon after the arrest of the martyrs, received a vivid account of the execution from somebody recently arrived in Douai from England, and included this information of an eye witness in his letter of 25 September 1600 to the Jesuit General (Jesuit General Archives, (Fondo Ges.) 651/614). This describes the large crowd of Catholics who gathered to witness the execution and who rushed forward to gather souvenirs and relics of the martyrs, and concludes, 'they ended their days by an illustrious martyrdom, which greatly edified the whole region'.

Father Robert Nutter and Father Edward Thwing were hanged, drawn and quartered at Lancaster on 26 July 1600, and were immediately recognised as martyrs by their fellow Catholics. The popular ballad, 'A Song of Four Priests' may not be great poetry, but it was published before 1616 and reflects accurately the understandings and feelings of the English Catholics of that time:

> In this our English coast much blessed blood is shed:
> Two hundred priests almost in our time martyred,
> And many lay-men die with joyful sufferance,
> Many more in prison lie, God's cause for to advance.
>
> Amongst this gracious troop, that follow Christ his train
> To cause the Devil stoop, four priests were lately slain:-
> Nutter's bold constancy and his sweet fellow, Thwing,
> Of whose most meek modesty angels and saints sing.
>
> Hunt's haughty courage stout, with godly zeal so true,
> Mild Middleton, but oh what tongue can half thy virtue
> shew!
> At Lancaster, lovingly, these martyrs took their end
> In glorious victory, true faith for to defend.

Thomas Palaser

Thomas Palaser was a man unable to avoid controversy. He did not seek it deliberately, but somehow, in his innocence, always seemed to get himself involved. Perhaps he tended to act too hastily and failed to foresee the full consequences of his actions, but at least he never wavered in his convictions and was resolute in defending himself against those who disagreed with what he did. He was not a political priest, but political circumstances pushed him into certain situations where he was obliged to make his own decisions in such delicate matters that he could not hope to have the universal approval of his contemporaries.

There is controversy even about his place of birth. He was certainly from the North Riding, but whether he was born in Ellerton-on-Swale or Kirby Wiske is a matter for disagreement. The Chalcedon returns of 1626 quote the statement of the Yorkshire attorney, Leonard Brackenbury that 'Mr Thomas Pallicer, priest (was) born at Ellerton super Swale in the parish of Bolton.' On the other hand, a Royal Pardon granted to Margaret Norton on 5 December, 1601, (Public Record Office, C 66/1591 mems. 26–27) is very clear in its reference to 'Thomas Palliser of Kirby Wiske in the county of Yorkshire, (who) was born at Kirby Wiske in the county of Yorkshire.' As Kirby Wiske is only eleven miles from Ellerton, the district is perhaps more important than the actual village. Such parish registers as might furnish more detail are missing, but his date of birth is calculated as 1570.

Nothing more is known of his early life until he presented himself at the English College at Rheims; the Douai Diary records his arrival on 24 July 1592. He did not stay long. Within a month he was sent to the new college which Father Robert Persons had opened in Valladolid, Spain, just three years before, and found himself projected at once into all the political turmoils of Spanish-English relationships. The Spaniards were still smarting from the defeat of the Armada in 1588 but King Philip II persisted in his plans for another invasion to further his own interests and to help the English Catholics. He had the full support of the Holy See, and, it would seem, a large measure of approval from the English Catholic exiles on the Continent. But a lot of English Catholics were strongly opposed to the idea of an armed invasion of their country to restore the Faith by force, and even Father Robert Persons, who had done so much to further the Spanish plans, could write in 1591 to the Spanish Secretary of State, 'God destroyed the Armada to preserve English Catholics, vho had already suffered so much from the heretics, from suffering still worse things at the hands of the Spaniards'.

It cannot have been an easy situation for Thomas Palaser to be lodged in the heart of Spain in such a political atmosphere. His Rector was a Spanish Jesuit; he was surrounded by Spaniards and most of the English Catholics he met were Spanish sympathisers. Only among his small group of fellow-students could he find Englishmen who shared his view that no Englishman should support the foreign invasion of his own country.

Thomas Palaser studied in Valladolid for three years. His date of enrolment was 3 January 1593, and he was ordained priest by the Archbishop of Burgos, sometime before February 1596. He then experienced some difficulty in obtaining a passage from a hostile Spain to England and it was not until the closing months of the year that his efforts achieved success.

Palaser himself has given the details of how he managed to leave Spain. In a letter of 18 March 1597 to William Waad, Clerk to the Privy Council (Cecil Papers, 39, f30), he explains that on the staff of the English College, Valladolid was a fellow-Yorkshireman, Father Charles Tancred SJ, who was also confessor to the Adelantado or Governor of Castile, Don Martin de Padilla. Father Tancred used his good offices to inform the Governor about Father Palaser's 'earnest desire to depart for my country', and the priest was summoned for an official interview. The meeting took place at Ferrol near Corunna on the north-west coast of Spain. Father Palaser obtained his passport, but was also commissioned by the Governor to help the Spanish cause by informing the Catholics of England of 'his sincere affection towards them, affirming that he intended nothing else, and that with an oath, but reformation of religion'.

In these circumstances, Thomas Palaser was enabled to return to England, but had the misfortune to be captured by the English very shortly after his arrival. By 12 March 1597 he was a prisoner in the Gatehouse, London, for on that date the Keeper of the Gatehouse presented the bill for his keep to the Exchequer, 'Thomas Palaser, a seminary priest, close prisoner doth owe for one week and six days . . . twenty nine shillings and eight pence'. (Catholic Record Society, vol. LIII, pp. 249–251).

Father Palaser was now in a quandary. As a loyal Englishman he had no love for the Spanish cause but he was being treated as a traitor by his own country. So he tried to prove his loyalty by giving the English Government such military information as he had been able to acquire in Spain by very astute observation. In his letter to William Waad, (quoted above) he told him that there were about six thousand Spanish soldiers at Ferrol and about four thousand more experienced soldiers at Bayona on the west coast of Spain. 'As touching the ships, there were in Ferrol about five and fifty, at the islands of Bayona about forty, great and little, the most of them in both places being Flemish hulks. I saw in Passage three new galleons with two new frigates, besides one or two old ships that there were. Further, it was said that at a place or port in Portugal called Portugalete, there were about eight galleons in making which would soon be ready'.

No professional secret agent could have produced better information and it was just what England needed. The Government, however showed little gratitude. Thomas Palaser was a priest and therefore a traitor and no good service to his country could obliterate his guilt. He was left in prison in the Gatehouse. His action however sparked off fierce controversy among the Catholics. In England, opinions were strongly divided; most of the continental exiles blamed him. The Spaniards were furious at what they regarded as the betrayal of their cause, and the officials of the Papal Court, who were trying so very hard to push the Spanish invasion forces into action, were highly indignant that an

English priest should act in this way.

There is a memorandum in the Vatican Library, (Cod. Lat. 6227, ff16r–17r) written to the Duke of Sesa, Spanish Ambassador at the Papal Court, and dated 16 August 1597. Its authorship is attributed to Monsignor Francisco Pena, Auditor of the Holy Roman Rota, but Father Robert Persons SJ is regarded as the real writer and certainly he pressed for the memorandum to be sent to Spain immediately.

This document blames Palaser for giving the English authorities information about Spanish preparations for an attack on England. It holds him and his disclosures responsible for the intensification of the persecution of the Catholics in the northern counties of England and also for the English expedition which destroyed the Spanish fleet at Cadiz.

It is unlikely that Palaser's confessions were the sole cause of the intensification of persecution in the north; it is quite unjust to hold him responsible for the raid on Cadiz which took place in June 1596, while he was still in Spain. The full force of the controversy could have little effect on Thomas Palaser in his prison, but on 29 May, in company with two other priests Father Francis Tillotson of Richmondshire and Father Robert Hawkesworth of Yorkshire, he escaped, leaving behind an unpaid bill for nine weeks accommodation at fourteen shillings per week. (Public Record Office, E 407/56, no. 342).

Once more Thomas Palaser found himself at the centre of a controversy, for in making his escape he had to break his parole. Now if there was one thing about the seminary priests that infuriated the Protestants more than any other it was the different understanding of what constitutes the truth. The Protestants expected plain, blunt truth; the Catholics used all their skill and knowledge of moral theology to preserve the truth while maintaining mental reservations and practicing equivocation. To the Protestants this was lying; to the Catholics it was truth.

Thomas Palaser was evidently aware of the uproar his escape would provoke, and he therefore left behind a letter of explanation. This letter, like his previous letter, was addressed to William Waad, the Clerk to the Privy Council and is dated c.29 May 1597 (Cecil Papers, 51, f52). Father Palaser pointed out that the Keeper of the Gatehouse, Mr Hugh Parlor, had tried to charge him eighteen pence so that four iron bars could be fitted to his cell window to make it more secure. Father Palaser had protested and it was then that he gave his promise, 'with an oath as I was a priest; that I would not depart'. Father Palaser did not deny that he had made his promise, but insisted that 'at which time I made the said promise, it was because of two evils the lesser should be accepted, that is to say, I chose rather so to do than to be chained up every night as I was'.

Mr Parlor did not accept his oath, claimed Father Palaser, 'as manifestly appears because he has placed John Smyth, his servant, in a chamber betwixt me and my other two brethren, lest we should break away. Therefore, I am cleared and quite discharged: for an oath not accepted of, although it be confirmed never so greatly, as also rashly made and without reason, does not bind in conscience'. So Father Palaser escaped, and as he stated did not find 'this course which I have taken anyway repugnant or prejudicial to my conscience'. He also gave another reason from common-sense and expediency. Crowds in the street had sent him messages, 'not only by speeches but very often by signs, that Topcliffe would procure my arraignment very shortly'. Topcliffe's interest in the case was quite enough to instil such fear in any victim as to deprive him of that freedom of choice required always in moral judgments.

Once more a free man, Thomas Palaser returned to the north of England and for the next three years busied himself as an active missionary priest. J.C.H. Aveling (*Northern Catholics*, p. 152–3) has picked up some traces of his presence in the North Riding, 'at Worsall, Northallerton (the Sayers), Osmotherley (a boy convert of his from there soon afterwards went abroad to become a priest), Lartington (another convert to be a priest) and South Otterington (the Talbots)'.

The Catholic Record Society gives at least more detail of these activities and possibly fresh information when it reports (Volume XXX pp. 60, 65, 81) that he reconciled to the Church three young Yorkshiremen, who later became students at the English College, Valladolid. Two of them, William Grange and Robert Appleby, became Benedictines in Spain and then returned as priests to the English mission. The third, Henry Killingham, became a Brother in the Society of Jesus in Spain.

Thomas Palaser was still working in Yorkshire when the Archpriest controversy broke out in 1598 and he was one of the priests who professed their loyalty to the Holy See and to the Archpriest, Father George Blackwell, by signing the letter to Pope Clement VIII.

Father Palaser was arrested for the second time on 24 June 1600. He was visiting a Catholic family at Ravensworth, but it is the Ravensworth in the parish of Lamesley near Gateshead and not the Ravensworth in Richmondshire. With the priest were his host, Mr John Norton of the famous Norton Conyers family, and his wife, as well as Mr Richard Sayer of Worsall, Yarm and Mr John Talbot of Thornton-le-Street in the North Riding. All were taken prisoner and brought to Durham where they were examined and committed to gaol. Toby Matthew, the Protestant Bishop of Durham reported the arrests in his letter of 27 June to Sir Robert Cecil and the Privy Council (Cecil Papers, 180, ff127rv and 128r). He calls Father Palaser 'a lusty, bold fellow' and adds the information that 'superstitious massing stuff and prohibited books belonging to the said priest' were found in the house. He also passes on Father Palaser's reminder to Cecil of the letter of explanation he had written at the time of his escape from the Gatehouse three years before.

Even in his arrest Thomas Palaser was not exempt from controversy, for this reminder of his to Sir Robert Cecil seemed to be an attempt to curry favour, and if so was conduct unbecoming a prospective martyr. This matter was much discussed by the investigators into his Cause, before it was accepted that the evidence was insufficient to prove that he had a base motive.

On 29 July 1600, Toby Matthew received his instructions from the Privy Council, (Acts of the Privy Council, XXX, London 1905, p. 543): 'Whereas there hath been a certain seminary priest taken of late in those parts by the labour and industry of Mr Sanderson, and some others apprehended also that did harbour and converse with him, because the said priest has lurked a long time in those parts, it is thought meet there should some care be taken to have both him and such others as have been apprehended very strictly examined of their behaviour and conversings, and then that such course be taken to proceed against them as shall be agreeable to law and you should think convenient'.

Father Cuthbert Trollope, another local priest working in the district at the same time, has left an extraordinary story of great detail about Father Palaser's experience in prison while awaiting trial. In the Chalcedon returns of 1626, he describes how 'they were like to have been poisoned by the malice of the gaoler', for the maid-servant twice brought them a mutton broth, which, by a miraculous sign they recognised as poisoned. The maid-servant was 'touched in conscience' and came on her knees to Mr Palaser to ask for forgiveness and he reconciled her to the Church.

The official records of the trial have been lost, but it took place at the Summer Assizes in Durham in early August, 1600. Contemporary Catholic sources are quite clear that the priest was charged under the statute of 1585 'against Jesuits, seminary priests and such other like disobedient persons'. Dr Thomas Worthington, President of Douai wrote in 1601, 'Another virtuous and learned priest called Palaser by like cruelty was judged and put to death at Durham, only for that he was a seminary priest and returned to his country contrary to the statute'. And Father Thomas Fitzherbert wrote in 1602 that he was condemned 'only for being a priest'.

Father Thomas Palaser found peace from his life of controversy by a cruel death. He was hanged, drawn and quartered at Durham on 8 September, 1600.

John Norton

It was in John Norton's house at Ravensworth near Gateshead that the priest Father Thomas Palaser was captured, and inevitably the host and his wife were among those accused of harbouring a priest and committed to Durham prison. According to Leonard Brackenbury in the Chalcedon Returns of 1626, John Norton was a Yorkshire gentleman and belonged to the family of Norton Conyers in the parish of Wath in the North Riding. In her learned article, 'Who was John Norton, the Martyr?' (*Recusant History*, April 1961, vol. 6, no. 2), Miss A.C.M. Foster has made an intensive study of the genealogy of this recusant family but is not able to answer her own question. She does however show the Catholic strength of the family with Richard Norton taking part in the Pilgrimage of Grace and no fewer than six Nortons actively engaged in the Earls' Rising of 1569, but the identity of John Norton the martyr continues to elude her.

Dr Foster has established that John Norton was not a recusant. She has searched the Recusant Rolls and every list of recusants so far discovered, but the name John Norton nowhere appears. It is this fact which leads her to make the suggestion that possibly the occasion of Father Palaser's visit to the house was to reconcile the whole family to the Church. Certainly this would account for the anger and confusion so vehemently shown when John Norton realised the full price that had to be paid for his reconciliation as the Government forces attacked his house.

John Norton was caught red-handed. He had a priest in the house; requisites for Mass were at hand. He attempted to protect the priest and evade arrest but all was in vain. Toby Matthew, Bishop of Durham in his report to Sir Robert Cecil (Cecil Papers

180, ff128–9r) gives a wonderful account of how the arrests were effected by the Government agent, Mr Henry Sanderson 'not without imminent peril of his life', for John Norton pursued him round the house firing off what can best be described as a blunderbuss. 'In the doing thereof one of my men present at that service thrust the said Norton with his rapier under the arm, whereby as God would, although he discharged the said piece, yet his aim and level failed'. Nevertheless, 'at the crack of the shot, every man there believed that Mr Sanderson had been slain'.

Arrested with John Norton was his wife Margaret as well as Mr John Talbot and Mr Richard Sayer, and of course Father Palaser. In Durham prison they were all offered their freedom if they would conform to the Established Church, but only Mr Sayer accepted. As Dr Thomas Worthington wrote (1601) 'the third gentleman, consenting of frailty to go to their church still lives, as the others might have done if they had also yielded'. This Richard Sayer had a proud record as a persistent recusant in Yarm but his courage failed him at the vital moment and he returned to his home as a free man. Within four years however, he was back in his rightful place in the Church for his name appears in E. Peacock's *List of Roman Catholics in the County of York in 1604*. Margaret Norton remained as steadfast as her husband and she too was condemned, but because she was with child she was immediately reprieved, and a year later, on 5 December 1601, was granted a Royal Pardon. (Public Record Office, C 66/1591, mems. 26–7). The wording of this Pardon is important because it states explicitly that she had been found guilty of a felony for harbouring a Catholic priest in contravention of the Statute of 1585 'against Jesuits, seminary priests and such other like disobedient persons'. In the absence of the official records of the trial, the nature of Margaret Norton's indictment proves that her husband, Father Palaser and Mr Talbot were all charged under the same Statute.

John Norton was executed at Durham in company with Father Thomas Palaser and Mr John Talbot on 8 September 1600. As a layman, he was spared the barbarism of being hanged, drawn and quartered but suffered death by simple hanging.

John Talbot

If John Norton's emergence as a recusant was rather sudden the same cannot be said about his companion in martyrdom, John Talbot, who must have been one of the best known recusants in the North Riding. His presence at Ravensworth with Father Thomas Palaser would seem to add strength to Dr Foster's theory that their purpose was to effect the reconciliation of John Norton.

Mr Leonard Brackenbury in the Chalcedon returns of 1626 states that John Talbot was born at Thornton-le-Street, which is a small village near South Kilvington and about one mile to the north of Thirsk. Father Cuthbert Trollope, Vicar General of the Northern District in 1625 calls him a 'Yorkshireman and gentleman'. Bishop Toby Matthew refers to him rather disparagingly as a 'yeoman'. Whatever his rank, he was a man of some wealth.

Father Hugh Bowler OSB has made a close study of the family (*Recusant History*, vol. 2, no. 1, p. 16) and shows that at the time of his father's death on 8 February 1573 the family estates at Thornton-le-Street, South Otterington and Sutton-under-Whitestone Cliffe extended over two thousand acres. John Talbot is not mentioned in his father's will and neither is the South Otterington property; evidently John had already been provided with these lands prior to his father's death. The family's pedigree was entered at the visitation of Yorkshire in 1612 by Richard St. George and again produced by Dugdale in 1666, but as Father Bowler points out it is curious that Dugdale ignores some of the work of his predecessor and fails to make any mention of John Talbot the martyr. This is due, he believes to a deliberate attempt to suppress his name. In the 1612 version it is clearly indicated that the third son has been omitted, for immediately after Thomas described as the second son, comes Richard described as the fourth son. If John is inserted in his proper place in the pedigree then he is the third son of John Talbot and his wife, formerly Alice Walker of Bedale. John himself was married to a lady called Ann but her maiden name is not known, and they seem to have had no male heir. It can be calculated from the Recusant Rolls of 1614 that John would be thirty-eight at the time of his death.

In another article, (*Recusant History*, vol. 2, no. 1, pp. 4–22) Father Bowler has used the Exchequer Dossiers to trace the course of John Talbot's recusancy. From this, it appears that he was first convicted of recusancy on 18 March 1587 when he was about twenty-five years of age. The fine of £140 (almost £3,000 in modern money) had not been paid and he persistently refused to attend the Anglican Church. No further action was taken against him until 1592, when the Barons of the Exchequer set up a Commission of Enquiry. The Commission met at Yarm on 17 April. Robert Rookeby and Humphrey Whorton presided over a group of Yorkshire gentlemen and a jury was sworn in. The Commissioners were not very enthusiastic and most reluctant to hurt in any way one of their neighbours, even though he be a Catholic. The result was that they invalidated all their actions by carelessly confusing Otterington with Otteringham in the East Riding. They also failed to notice the very common recusant practice of transferring their land to non-recusants for a time so that they could claim they had no wealth to pay their fines.

The case dragged on into more and more complicated legal proceedings, and Father Bowler comments how ill-served the Crown authorities were by the Yorkshire Commissioners and jurors. 'The fact is surely not without its significance. Many of the latter were probably acquaintances, even friends of the victims; it should not therefore surprise us to find indications that they reacted to their enforced participation in the operation of the recusancy laws with some disgust. Even at Yarm, their efforts, if we may judge by the inaccuracy of the verdict and the absence of any assessment of John's goods and chattels (all of which should have been forfeited to the Crown) had been conspicuously lacking in zeal'. (*Recusant History*, vol. 2, no. 1, p. 9).

Meanwhile of course, while the legal case continued John Talbot escaped paying his fines, and it was not until five years later that the matter was brought to a conclusion when John himself appeared before the Court of the Exchequer and won his case on a point of law. Within two years, however, John Talbot was in trouble again for refusing to attend the Anglican Church and on 2 April 1599 was convicted and fined £60. The details of his subsequent arrest at Ravensworth on 24 June 1600 have already been given in the accounts of Father Thomas Palaser and Mr John Norton. It should however be added here that John Talbot also made a bid to protect his priest. Leonard Brackenbury in the Chalcedon returns of 1626 states precisely that he 'lost his life for being in the priest's company and drawing his sword. The Judge asked him why he drew it; he answered, "in our defence". And so was brought within the compass of the law for harbouring the priest'.

John Talbot, like his companions, was offered his life if he would conform to the Established Church. After so many years of such determined recusancy he could make only one answer to that suggestion and his acceptance of death was the culmination of a lifetime's fidelity to the Catholic Church.

John Talbot was hanged at Durham on 8 September, 1600.

Robert Middleton

Was Robert Middleton the brother of Saint Margaret Clitherow? The eminent Catholic historian, Joseph Gillow, had no doubts and places Robert as a younger son of Thomas Middleton, whose daughter Margaret married the York butcher John Clitherow in 1571, and was canonised in 1970. Gillow's contemporaries are not so certain. Father John Hungerford Pollen SJ, Editor of the Catholic Record Society's Volume 5 in 1908, quoted Gillow's assertion but expressed his own doubts and those of another outstanding Catholic scholar of the time, Father John Morris SJ. Of the more modern Catholic historians, Father Godfrey Anstruther OP makes no mention of the alleged relationship in his account of the life of Robert Middleton in Volume 1 of *The Seminary Priests* (1968), and J.C.H. Aveling remarks in *Catholic Recusants in the City of York* (p. 73) only that it is possible that Margaret Clitherow's 'blood relations, the Middletons produced a seminary priest, Robert Middleton'.

Both Anstruther and Aveling have helped Miss Mary Claridge to produce a genealogy of the Middletons as Appendix 3 to her standard work on Margaret Clitherow (1966). Nowhere do they accept that Robert was a brother of Margaret. They name the five children of Thomas Middleton and include a Margaret but no Robert. They note that among these five children was another Thomas, but query that he was the father of Robert. They also find another Thomas Middleton, a tanner, who died in the parish of All Saints, North Street in 1572, leaving children Peter, Robert and Anne about whom nothing else is yet known; this Robert might possibly be Robert the martyr. All in all, it seems extremely doubtful therefore that Robert Middleton could be the brother of Margaret Clitherow. He might be her nephew, but prudently the Documents for the Cause of Robert Middleton make no reference to her.

The best information about Robert Middleton is evidence from his own mouth, and it is fortunate that the details of his examination before Sir Richard Houghton and Mr Thomas Hesketh at Preston on 30 September 1600 are readily available. (Public Record Office SP 12/275 no. 83). In this examination, Robert Middleton admitted that he 'was born in the county of York and was the son of Thomas Middleton of the said City'. He gave his age as thirty-one years, and described how he had been educated in York until he had reached the age of eighteen, during which time, 'he thinketh he did go usually to church, but after that time he refused to go to church, and being asked who persuaded him from the church, he sayeth he cannot tell other than his own conscience and the reading of books'.

Robert Middleton gave more details of his early life but was careful not to incriminate others. He had a convenient memory which grew very vague when questions were asked about names and on certain matters he refused point-blank to answer. He described how he had spent six or seven years in London and then some time in Hull, but found himself unable to remember where he stayed. Nor could he remember the names of his companions. 'Afterwards, having a purpose to go to one of the seminaries at Douai or at Rome', he took ship from Hull and landed at Calais, but he refused to name the ship and said merely that it was a ship from Newcastle carrying coals to Calais. From Calais, he journeyed to Douai and stayed there three years. He offered the information that Dr Richard Barrett was the President of the College at that time, but then Dr Barrett had died the previous year and was beyond the powers of the Court. When asked what other Englishmen lived at the College, Robert Middleton said bluntly 'He would not answer'.

He made no attempt to disguise the fact that he was a priest. He said he had lived in the English College at Rome for one year and that he had been ordained priest by a Bishop, whose name he had now forgotten. He admitted that he had an interview with the Pope before setting out for England but he could not remember the names of his travelling companions. He had crossed the seas in a Dutch ship from Flushing to the south of England, but would not name his port of arrival and refused to give any account at all about his subsequent movements or the people who had befriended him. Nevertheless, he told the Court that he had said Mass, christened children, married people and reconciled others to the Church of Rome, 'doing all other things concerning a priest'. Robert Middleton professed his loyalty to the Queen but avoided the trick question as to what he would do if the Pope invaded England. Then he decided that he had said enough and refused to answer any more questions. All this information was sent to Sir Robert Cecil and the Privy Council by Sir Richard Houghton on 1 October 1600.

Contemporary Catholic sources have little to add. The Douai Diary was not kept properly between the years 1593–8, but it is known (from Catholic Record Society vol. XXXVII, p. 105) that in 1597 Robert Middleton was twenty-six years of age when he entered the Venerable English College, Rome, and therefore by calculation he was born in 1571 and studied at Douai from 1594 to 1597. Aveling has produced evidence, (*Catholic Recusancy in York*, p. 72) that among the Catholic youths leaving York in 1584–5 for education overseas were Robert Middleton and Henry Clitherow, but again this reference would seem to be to another Robert Middleton. Brother H. Foley SJ, (*Records of the English Province of the Society of Jesus*, vol. vii, p. 1367) has shown that Robert Middleton moved from Douai to Rome on 14 April 1597 and the Register of Ordinations for the Roman Vicariate gives his date of ordination at the German College as 4 January 1598. He set out for the English Mission on 20 April. (Catholic Record Society, vol. XXXVII, p. 105).

The Bishop of Chalcedon and many others have claimed that Father Robert Middleton was a student of the English College at Seville, but this is quite mistaken and is the result of an error in Dr Thomas Worthington's catalogue of 1614.

As a priest in England, Father Middleton worked in Yorkshire and Lancashire. He had the misfortune to be captured within two years by Lord Burghley (Thomas Cecil) President of the Council of the North and the elder brother of Sir Robert Cecil. Lord Burghley lived at Snape near Bedale in the North Riding and his letter to Sir Robert Cecil of 8 January 1600 (Public

Record Office, SP 12/274, no.10) reported, 'This Christmas I have taken in a house at Ripon, within six miles of my house at Snape, two notorious seminaries. . . . (Martin) Nelson and (Robert) Middleton', and he added about Robert Middleton that he was 'very well learned and a very stout and resolute fellow'. The prisoners were taken to York, where Father Martin Nelson, a Yorkshireman from Overton in the North Riding, conformed to the established Church and received a pardon. Robert Middleton, however, stood firmly by his faith and then managed to escape from custody, although no details are known.

For the next nine months Robert Middleton worked, it would seem, in Lancashire before he was again caught on 30 September 1600 on the highway at the Fylde near Preston. His captor, Sir Richard Houghton, a Justice of the Peace, informed Sir Robert Cecil in his letter of 1 October 1600 (Public Record Office, SP 12/275, no. 83) that 'Yesterday I apprehended a seminary priest in the way that leadeth into a part of Lancashire called the Fylde. The priest was well-horsed and appointed with his pistol. There was with him one other man, who escaped from me and as yet I cannot find him. The priest that is apprehended names himself Robert Middleton. He had no letters nor any other thing of importance found upon him, saving only a popish service book. He had in his purse forty shillings or thereabouts, which I have suffered him to keep for his maintenance in prison, and have already sent him to the Castle at Lancaster.' An account has been preserved by Father Christopher Grene in his Collection M (printed in Catholic Record Society, vol. V, p. 388). It is of unknown authorship but the date is accepted as 1601: 'Mr Middleton was apprehended by Sir Richard Houghton in the highway in Lancashire, who asking of this good man what he was, he told him plainly that he was a priest, and so to all such questions directly he answered the plain truth'.

After his examination already described, Father Middleton was taken under escort from Preston to Lancaster Castle, and on the way there occurred the sort of event which the modern reader would associate more with the Wild West of America than with the ordinary vicissitudes of recusant priests. A group of Catholics made an attempt to rescue the priest from the hands of his captors.

Henry Breres, a draper of Preston, one of the guards responsible for Father Middleton, gave an eye-witness account of what happened in his testimony before the Mayor of Preston, Mr Henry Hodgkinson, on 2 October 1600. (Public Record Office, SP 12/275, no. 115). Mr Breres stated that he had been commanded by the Mayor to join Mr Henry Sudell and Mr Edmund Machon in escorting the prisoner to Lancaster Castle, but when they were about five miles out of Preston they were passed on the road by a group of four horsemen. A few minutes later, these horsemen returned at the gallop, and pulling up their horses, asked, 'Is this prisoner a priest?' Henry Breres' immediate response was to grab hold of Father Middleton to prevent his escape. Whereupon, the four horsemen drew their swords and attacked the escort. A running fight ensued, but Breres held on to his prisoner.

One of the attacking force, (Greenlowe, says Breres, but in reality another priest, Father Thurstan Hunt) drew his pistol and pulled the trigger but the weapon failed to fire. James Dike seized the opportunity to pull Greenlowe off his horse and seeing this the other assailants fled. Greenlowe resisted furiously and managing to break loose from those who held him, took to his heels to follow his companions. He was pursued for over a mile by three of the escort but they dare not approach him too closely for fear of his pistol and had to content themselves with throwing stones. Meanwhile, the priest had put his pistol in order again and firing off four bullets wounded one of his pursuers in the thigh. It became something like the legend of Custer's last stand. Eventually the priest was overcome by sheer weight of numbers, and now there were two priests in custody instead of one.

The rescue attempt was an act of heroism but it was an error of judgement. The violence offered by the Catholic party caused more harm than good. The whole operation was a failure, but worse than this it served to antagonise the civil authorities and many Catholics suffered as a result. The incident and its consequences are described by Father Richard Blount SJ in a letter to Father Richard Persons on 22 October 1600 (Grene's Collection M). He begins his letter in Catholic code assuring Father Persons that 'we are all well and follow our accustomed trade with good profit, for our customers (thanks be to God) do daily increase'. He then goes on to report, 'The persecution was never more hot than at this moment. . . There is a priest taken in Lancashire recently, and being sent to gaol, by the way, an attempt was made to have rescued him by four of that country, but being too weak, one of the four was taken, and much matter is given hereby to the Chief Justice to speak out against all recusants, which he has done to Her Majesty in the highest degree'.

The rescue attempt and violence also affected the way in which the two captive priests were treated by the authorities. The anonymous author of the Catholic document of 1601 describes 'the harsh conditions of their imprisonment as they were taken to Lancaster under double guard, where they were hardly handled, being loaded with irons night and day. And so remained till they were sent up to London, and that in most severe manner: for they had but very ill horses scant able to go, their legs were tied under the horses belly, their diet was very bad, and every night they were parted and their legs bolted to the bed stock'.

Father Robert Middleton and Father Thurstan Hunt were sent to London because the Privy Council was alarmed 'that some others of that corrupted seed did forcibly attempt the rescuing' (Acts of the Privy Council, XXX, London 1905, pp. 720–721). 'We think it fit to have it thoroughly examined who were the rest of the confederates in so great an insolency, which we find needs special redress and reformation in those parts, being grown to so intolerable a boldness. . . We do therefore pray and require you the Sheriff to cause as well as the said Middleton as the said Greenlowe to be sent up hither, bound under some convenient guard'.

In London, Middleton and Hunt (Greenlowe) were committed to the Gatehouse and kept in close confinement for the next four months. They were formally examined many times and finally one day as they prepared to go to the bar for another examination, they found to their surprise 'a number of men with weapons and horses ready to conduct them back again' (to Lancashire). They asked permission to go back to their chamber to collect their personal belongings but the keeper said, 'This that you have will serve your turn, for the time you have to live is very short'. (Anonymous document of 1601, Catholic Record Society, vol. V, pp. 388–390).

It was while he was in prison in London that Father Robert

Middleton became a Jesuit. A letter of Father Henry Garnett SJ dated 30 June 1599 provides evidence of Middleton's request to join the Society, but this letter was intercepted by the Government and never delivered. In another letter, however, of 11 March 1601, Father Garnett informs the Jesuit General, Father Claudius Aquaviva, that he has told Father Middleton that his request to become a Jesuit has been granted (Foley, *Records of English Province SJ*, vol. VII, p. 963).

Back in Lancaster, Father Robert Middleton and Father Thurstan Hunt were brought to trial at the Lent Assizes in 1601. No official records of the trial are in existence but Catholic sources are quite clear that they were charged under the Statute of 1585 'Against Jesuits, seminary priests and such other like disobedient persons'. Dr Thomas Worthington (1601) says, 'They were so condemned and executed merely for their priesthood', and Father Thomas Fitzherbert, (1602) numbers them with a group of others 'all of them martyred only for being Catholic priests'.

The anonymous document of 1601 gives some details of Father Middleton's last day on earth. He gave away many of his personal goods to be distributed to his friends. He effected the reconciliation of the criminals who were to die with him. He spoke cheerfully to those who visited him and reproached his sister who was prepared to offer £100 for his release. 'In all Lancaster', continues this document, 'there could not be found any that would either lend their horses or cart or hurdle or any such like thing for their death, so the Sheriff was fain to take one of his own horses to draw the sledge'.

Father Robert Middleton and Father Thurstan Hunt were brought to execution together. They both appeared on the scaffold wearing their priestly cassocks. They embraced each other as brothers and each knelt for the other's blessing. Then they were hanged, drawn and quartered. The 1601 document states that many Catholics were present to witness the martyrdom, and then concludes. 'Everyone lamented their death, for all the world perceived their innocence, and not only Catholics but schismatics and of all sorts strived to have something of theirs for relics'.

Father Middleton's recognition as a martyr was immediate. The many Catholic witnesses to his death passed on the message to their fellow Catholics in other parts of England and on the Continent. Such was the popularity of his Cause that he is named in the well known 'Ballad of Four Priests' of 1616. The poet calls him 'mild Middleton', but seems to have chosen his adjective more for its alliterative effect than as a true characteristic of an extraordinary man of fierce determination.

Many sources say the martyrdom took place in March 1601 but the Chalcedon Catalogue of 1628 seems to be more accurate in giving an exact date of 3 April. The official Documents of the Cause have settled for the statement, 'about 3rd April, 1601.'

Matthew Flathers

When Queen Elizabeth died in the West Country on 24 March 1603, the hopes of English Catholics were at once raised that the accession of the new King, James Stuart, the son of Mary Queen of Scots, would usher in a period of religious toleration. James had already made several vague promises on the subject and he was known to be a gentle scholar and man of peace, but his Catholic baptism was insufficient to curb his Protestant education and he made no attempt to remove the Penal Laws from the Statute Book. Nevertheless, the pressure on Catholics was lessened, and certainly in the early years of his reign the King sought to banish the priests rather than to execute them.

A Royal Proclamation on 22 February 1604 ordered the expulsion of all priests from the Kingdom, and this Order was repeated on 10 June 1606. The result of this legislation was a coming and going of priests across the seas as those who were banished returned in secret almost immediately to resume their interrupted apostolate. Amid all this confusion there arrived in England Father Matthew Flathers, recently ordained but already about forty-six years of age.

Matthew Flathers had been born at Weston near Otley in the West Riding of Yorkshire, according to the Chalcedon Catalogue of 1628. From the Douai Diary it appears that his year of birth was 1560, but the Records of Oxford University suggest a date four years later. He was probably the youngest son of John and Agnes Flathers, who had a family of six sons and two daughters. He is described in the Registers of the University of Oxford as a yeoman or the son of a commoner. (Boase and Clark, II, ii, p. 146). He was twenty-one years of age when he matriculated on 2 July 1585, and as a member of University College he was admitted to the degree of B.A. on 27 February 1590. Presumably he left Oxford after graduation but there are no signs that he was in any way a Catholic.

Sometime within the next fourteen years he must have been reconciled to the church. He presented himself at Douai on 18 August 1604 and was permitted to begin his studies for the priesthood even though he was at least forty years of age. On 22 March 1605 he received the sacrament of Confirmation from the Bishop of Arras and used this occasion to change his first name from Maior to Matthew. So far in the English College he was on probation and paying his own way, but in June of the same year he was enrolled as an alumnus and was supported at the College's expense. Matthew Flathers was a mature student and his theology course lasted less than two years. He was ordained priest on Holy Saturday, 25 March 1606, as the Douai Diary reports, with four others at Arras, and on 30 June he set out for the English Mission.

Within a short time of his arrival in his home country he was captured. Charles Dodd, (*Church History of England*, 1739) reports that he was apprehended and condemned to death for receiving Catholic Orders overseas, but that he then had his sentence changed to perpetual banishment, and found himself back in France only a few months after his first departure.

Father Flathers joined the procession of banished priests recrossing the Channel and once more made his way to his native Yorkshire, where he was captured at Upsall Castle, South Kilvington, near Thirsk, in August 1607. Indeed, Father Flather's very brief priestly life seems to have consisted of several periods of 'a few months': a few months of freedom in England then a few months in prison; then banishment and return; a few more months freedom, and then a few months in prison in York before his death. His whole career as a priest lasted less than twenty-four months.

Upsall Castle, once one of the ancient homes of the Scrope family was at this time owned by the Constables and had been for many years a safe house of rest and refuge for the missionary priests. There had been trouble in 1592–3 when Father Thomas Clarke was captured and had then turned Queen's evidence to incriminate his brethren. (Aveling, *Northern Catholics*, p. 161). Many priests suffered as a result, and Lady Constable only escaped the powers of the law by court influence. Instead, her brother-in-law, Joseph Constable (who kept his own refuge for priests at nearby Kirkby Knowle Castle) was indicted in absentia and lived as an outlaw for five years. Nevertheless, Aveling maintains that Upsall Castle continued to be used by priests throughout the 1590s, and he refers in particular to the safety of the building with its maze of vaults and cellars where priests could hide before making their escape into the surrounding countryside and the beckoning moors. Father Flathers should have been safe at Upsall Castle, and indeed would have been safe had it not been for the machinations of a certain Sir Stephen Procter, who was constantly on the hunt for Catholic priests and spent his days following up every possible opportunity to make his captures.

Stephen Procter was a trouble-maker. Having bought Fountains Abbey from the Greshams in 1597, he then proceeded to annoy his neighbours by tearing down the old Abbot's lodgings to build his own mansion. He was involved in tedious litigation with most of his neighbours over land rights, and among them were the good Catholics Sir William Ingleby, Sir John Mallory and Sir John Yorke. It was in order to attack these neighbours that Procter made every use of the recusancy laws and pursued priests with such personal hatred.

At a later trial February, 1614, Sir Stephen Procter gave a full account of his raid on Upsall Castle. (Public Record Office, Star Chamber, 8/18/1 f118). He boasted first of his great success in capturing Father Christopher Wharton at Ripley Park and rejoiced at his subsequent execution at York on 28 March 1600. He then describes how he and Sir Timothy Whattingham, with Thomas Jackson and Gerard Birkhead, 'by continual search and watch, both night and day, for the space of several days and nights together, to the great charge and peril of their lives, at last found and apprehended within the Castle of Upsall in the North Riding, two other seminary priests there hidden in the secret vaults or caves of the said Castle. The one called Mush, a supposed confederate in the said Gunpowder treason and much given to frequenting Nidderdale, and the other called Flathers, and a third prelate supposed to be Gerrard, directly touched with the Gunpowder Treason, and which said third person, supposed to be Gerrard, did then suddenly in the night at a back door of the said Castle break out, giving the watchman there present a sudden blow, whereby whilst the watchman was stunned the said third person escaped, but the said two other priests being so taken were conducted by this defendant to the said Council in the North'. So much for Sir Stephen Procter. His details of the planning of the raid are interesting, but he confuses the names of the priests. The third priest, who escaped, was not Father John Gerard SJ but Father Cuthbert Trollope from County Durham. Father Mush was Father William Mush, the younger brother of the better known Father John Mush.

Father Flathers and Father Mush were taken to York for trial, and as Father Richard Holtby reported on 13 April 1608 in a letter to Father Robert Persons SJ (Roman Archives SJ, Anglia 37, f130r) they were both condemned, 'together with the gentlewoman in whose house they were taken'. This 'gentlewoman' may have been a lady from a distance in residence to look after the priests but it is more likely that it was Lady Constable herself. Father John Mush in a letter of 27 April 1608 to Pope Paul V (Westminster Diocesan Archives, B, XXIV no. 27), refers to the prisoner as a widow, and at the time of his writing Lady Constable was indeed a widow, having lost her husband Sir Henry Constable on 15 December 1607. Whoever this lady was, she continued in prison, adamant in her refusal to take the Oath until she was eventually reprieved and released.

Father William Mush also persisted in his refusal to take the Oath but for some unknown reason he was reprieved from the death sentence, and then, following the family tradition, made his escape. A rumour that Father William Mush had been martyred reached the English College and is recorded in the Douai Diary. His 'martyrdom' was also reported to the Apostolic Nuncio in Paris by Father John Cecil in May 1608, but the facts of his escape are well established and the Calendar of State Papers for 1608 records that William Wharton, the keeper of the gaol at York Castle, was fined £250 at York Assizes 'for suffering William Mush, a convicted seminary priest to escape out of the said gaol'.

For Father Flathers there was no escape and no reprieve. No

official record of his trial has survived but the Third Douai Diary makes clear (Catholic Record Society, vol. X, p. 90) that he was sentenced to death because he was a priest and then executed because he refused to take the Oath. The Archpriest, Father George Birkhead, informed Pope Paul V on 21 June 1608 (Westminster Diocesan Archives, A VIII p. 337) that Father Matthew Flathers was one of the three priests who had that year suffered martyrdom for defending 'the true Faith regarding the new oath'.

Father Flathers died in great agony. Even for a seminary priest his execution was particularly horrifying. Father James Pollard SJ who may well have been an eye witness, reported some of the details in his letter of 1610 (Stoneyhurst manuscripts Anglia, III, no.100), and claims that the spectacle of cruelty was such as to 'move many to commiseration of us and our cause'.

Matthew Flathers was hanged, drawn and quartered outside Micklegate Bar at the Knavesmire, York on 21 March, 1608.

Thomas Atkinson

'The year 1609 passed without the shedding of any Catholic blood for religious matters: a thing to be remarked, because the like had not happened since the year 1580'. So wrote Bishop Richard Challoner in 1741 (*Memoirs of Missionary Priests*, 1924 edition, p. 299), and he was of course referring to the whole of England. In Yorkshire however this truce in religious persecution lasted for many years, and indeed during the next forty years, from the execution of Father Matthew Flathers in 1608 to the execution at York in 1642 of Blessed John Lockwood and Blessed Edward Catherick, only two Yorkshiremen were called upon to give their lives for their Faith. One of these was Blessed Thomas Tunstall OSB, whose family lived at Wycliffe and who was hanged, drawn and quartered at Norwich on 13 July 1616; the other was Father Thomas Atkinson, one of the oldest and most experienced priests of the English Mission, who for twenty-eight years had roamed across Yorkshire from Richmondshire to Howdenshire ministering to the needs and religious comfort of the small, scattered Catholic communities.

Catholic historians are not certain as to where Thomas Atkinson was born, but they all agree that he was a Yorkshireman by birth. The Chalcedon Catalogue of 1616 says he was born at Leeds in the West Riding; Father John Knaresborough (*Sufferings of the Catholics*, c.1720) says he was born in the East Riding. Bishop Challoner accepts the East Riding. Of the more recent historians, Father Godfrey Anstruther OP (*Seminary Priests*, vol. 1, p. 13) states that Atkinson was born in the East Riding but then goes on to use the Jesuit General Archives to advance the claims of Leeds. J.C.H. Aveling (*Northern Catholics*, p. 173), refers to the Atkinson family of Richmond and points out that William Atkinson was the father of a seminary priest, another William Atkinson of Valladolid, but then adds, 'It is possible that William had another priest son, Thomas Atkinson, the martyr, who worked most of his priestly life in the East Riding'. Aveling makes another reference to a Father Atkinson in his work on the East Riding, (*Post-Reformation Catholicism in East*

Yorks, p. 22). He calls him Father William Atkinson, but from the context it is clear that he means Thomas and he describes him as 'another Douai priest and native of the (East) Riding'.

The official Documents of the Cause do not settle the matter. They state very prudently that Thomas Atkinson was born in Yorkshire, either at Leeds or somewhere in the East Riding and give his date of birth as about 1545.

Thomas Atkinson must have been nearly forty years of age when he arrived at the English College at Rheims to begin his studies for the Priesthood. His arrival is not recorded in the Douai Diary but the probable date was 1585. The Diary does record his ordination to the Priesthood at Laon on 11 June 1588, and his departure for the English Mission on the 11th November following.

Father Atkinson returned to Yorkshire and formed a working partnership with another priest, Blessed William Andleby (or Anlaby), who came from Etton near Market Weighton on the very fringes of the Howdenshire area and who had already spent ten years on the Yorkshire mission. Professor John Bossy, (*The English Catholic Community*, 1975, p. 253) describes their work: 'Anlaby started in 1578, tramping with his kit in a bag, then bought a horse and joined up with Atkinson, with whom he served an extensive territory running from Richmond to Hull. Anlaby was arrested in 1597, and so apparently was the horse, for Atkinson thereafter went the round on foot until his own arrest. . .' J.C.H. Aveling in recounting the same information adds the detail that 'they ranged widely from Richmond through York to Howden, Hemingbrough and Hull'. (*Post-Reformation Catholicism in East Yorks*, p. 22).

The zeal and industry of the two priests is commended by Bishop Richard Challoner (*Missionary Priests*, 1924 edition, p. 232) and he gives an example from the writings of Dr Champney (1618): 'Whereas many Catholics were kept prisoners for their conscience in Hull Castle, and no one was allowed to have access to them, or speak to them, otherwise than in the presence of the keeper, who was a bitter enemy of their religion, Mr Andleby and Mr Atkinson, with incredible labour and danger, in spite of moats and walls, gates and bars, found means several times to come at them, and to comfort and assist them'.

One detects here the influence on their work of the layman Blessed Thomas Warcopp, with whom Father Andleby was closely associated and at whose home at Gatenby near Burneston, between Boroughbridge and Catterick, he was finally arrested in 1597. Mr Warcopp was well known for his skill in getting in and out of prisons and had devised special means of avoiding the guards and circumventing locked doors and formidable physical barriers.

The arrest of Father Andleby and his subsequent martyrdom left Father Atkinson on his own, but he continued to serve the same territory walking from place to place. Indeed, 'travelling on foot' is a phrase used constantly by his contemporaries to describe his activities. The *Exemplar Literarum* (1616) describes how this elderly priest frequently passed whole nights without sleep, 'either employed in the functions of his ministry or in his journeys: for by serving the same parts of the country for so many years, he was become so well known to the heretics that he could not safely travel by day'. And Bishop Richard Challoner quotes this same document to explain how he worked, 'going always on foot, and for the most part by night, from one Catholic house to another, to help, confess and administer the sacraments'. (*Memoirs of Missionary Priests*, 1924 edition, Part 2, 1742, p. 89).

Father Atkinson was inevitably a frequent visitor at Lady Grace Babthorpe's house at Osgodby in Howdenshire, and in her Memoirs of 1620 she wrote, 'There was a good priest, one Mr Atkinson, in our country, who lived long in doing great service to God, taking great pains in serving the poor, which without such pains could not have had those helps and comforts that they should need of in these times. For divers years, he travelled a foot, enduring all weathers, and many times when he had had a weary and wet day, the houses to which he went could not receive him in, but that he must stay in some out-house or corner, he being both wet and cold, and in time of frost and snow, to such time as the owners of the houses could for their safety receive him in.

'Another charity the good man used, which was that when he came to the poor folk's houses, he would not let them be at any charge, but both find himself meat and them, and give them money too, so that what he received of those that were able, he bestowed on the poor'. A little later in her Memoirs, Lady Babthorpe relates a significant incident in the life of Father Atkinson, when 'In a great frost, he got a fall and broke his leg, in the cure of which he suffered much, lighting on an evil surgeon. Yet after his recovery, he used his former charity and pains, but not able to travel a foot much, had a horse to help him.'

In his early days on the Mission, probably about 1589, Father Atkinson heard the first confession of an eight year old boy, Robert Watkinson of Menthorpe near Hemingbrough, and so played his part in preparing another Yorkshireman for the martyr's crown. This boy was later educated at secret Catholic schools, first at Castleford and then at Richmond, before proceeding to Douai and Rome to be ordained priest in March 1602. He was martyred at Tyburn on 20 April 1602, within the first month of his ordination, when only twenty-three years of age, and is now recognised by the Church as Blessed Robert Watkinson.

Father John Knaresborough, in his book 'The Sufferings of the Catholics', (c.1720 Humberside Record Office, DDEV/67/1 p. 211) also used the *Exemplar Literarum* of 1616 to comment on the quality and length of Father Atkinson's apostolate. He writes, 'As his zeal for the conversion of souls was remarkable, so was his prudence and discretion highly commendable in the cautious management of his business, so as not to expose himself to unnecessary dangers: which under God, was the cause that kept him out of the hands of the persecutors for thirty years together, during the worst of times, wherein he had seen many of his brethren missioners fall a sacrifice to the fury of these bloody persecutions. With these precautions, Mr Atkinson weathered many a storm during the greatest and worst part of Queen Elizabeth's and King James's reigns, and succeeded so well as to spin out his life to the 70th year of his age and the 30th of his mission in England, a thing very uncommon in those evil days'.

For Father Atkinson to preserve his freedom for so long was an extraordinary achievement in the circumstances of those days, especially as he was so well known to so many people over a wide area. Nor did his distinctive limp in later years do much to help him in his attempts to conceal his identity. Yet no reference to him as a priest has ever been found in the reports of spies or in any official document. He must have been known to many people who were not friendly to the Catholic Church but they respected this lonely priest and shut their eyes to his religious activities, because they appreciated he was a man who 'went about doing good'.

Father Atkinson was caught, still in Howdenshire, early in 1616, when he paid a visit to the Vavasour family at Willitoft near Bubwith. This cadet branch of the Vavasour family of Hazlewood had been established in Spaldington since 1481, and according to F.H. Sunderland, (*Life of Lord Langdale*, c.1938) they had acquired by marriage the neighbouring estate of Willitoft. They were known in the sixteenth century as 'Roman Catholics of the worst sort' when even the Askes of Aughton were labelled as 'less evil'. To such a family Father Atkinson must have been a regular visitor, but on this occasion he arrived with the foreknowledge that all was not well and that his own capture was imminent. A letter dated 17 June 1616 from an unnamed Jesuit priest in York to Father Joseph Creswell SJ (Jesuit Roman Archives, Anglia, 37, ff80v) relates that 'a day before Mr Atkinson was taken he had his vision. Being in prayer and commending to God the end of his old age, that he might die in his grace, he had an inward answer saying that he should quickly have occasion to suffer for his sake . . . the next day, he was taken and very hardly used'. The *Exemplar Literarum* gives the additional information that Our Lady had appeared to Father Atkinson, told him of his coming fate and encouraged him to fortitude.

It is difficult to see why, after so many years of friendship, the local Protestants should suddenly turn against Father Atkinson. There is no evidence of an intensification of the persecution on a national scale and no evidence of unexpected directives from the authorities in York. Perhaps local animosities played their part, but whatever the reason Father Atkinson was seen and reported, and the report was acted upon. A hostile neighbour observed his arrival at the Vavasour house and next morning, as he was leaving, the pursuivants were waiting for him and he was arrested. At the same time, Mr Peter Vavasour and his wife and children were also arrested, and all were taken to York with the priest. The letter of the unnamed Jesuit, (quoted above) describes the journey to York: 'They took all they found about him and carried him a-horseback, bound hand and foot to prison, without a cloak in a very cold time, and did him many other injuries, which he suffered patiently'.

In prison, Father Atkinson was closely questioned, presumably by the members of the Council of the North. His treatment was very harsh; no attention was paid to his age. He was urged to take the oath of allegiance of 1606, which would have secured freedom, but he steadfastly refused all such persuasions and remained constant in his Faith.

It was while he was in prison that God showed him another special favour. Both the *Exemplar Literarum* and Lady Grace Babthorpe testify that while Father Atkinson was at prayer, the irons which pinioned his legs fell miraculously to the ground. 'This being reported', wrote Lady Babthorpe, 'the Lord Sheffield, who was then President, sent for the keeper to know if it were true, who confessed the truth'.

The trial took place at the Lent Assizes in York, but no official records have survived. Catholic sources however are clear that he was charged under the Statute of 1585, 'against Jesuits, seminary priests and such other like disobedient persons'. Questioned as to his priesthood, Father Atkinson refused to answer; he knew well that to acknowledge that he was a priest would endanger the lives of the whole Vavasour family who already stood accused of 'harbouring a priest'. He would not admit his priesthood, but at the same time he would not deny it. 'Therefore he desired not to be urged any more with those questions, which he conceived he was not obliged to answer', wrote Father John Knaresborough.

It was difficult for the Court to prove the fact of his priesthood. Even though many people knew him to be a priest, they refused to come forward to testify against him. But then the pursuivants produced his rosary beads, some grains of incense and a copy of a papal indulgence, all of which they had found on his person; and this evidence, coupled to the fact that he would not deny he was a priest, was sufficient for the jury to find him guilty and the judges to sentence him to death.

Whilst in prison awaiting execution, Father Atkinson was

visited several times by the unknown Jesuit priest who wrote the letter of 1616 to Father Joseph Creswell SJ. It was a time of strained relationships between the Jesuits and the secular clergy, but Father Atkinson had always been close to the Jesuits and was one of the few seminary priests to hold them in high regard. 'He was always very intrinsical with ours', wrote the Jesuit, a little cryptically, and 'in testimony of his love bestowed his books and other things of his on me and other Fathers of ours, his acquaintances. I often visited him in prison and was near him when he died and he seemed glad to see me there. He recounted unto me in prison the vision with all the circumstances of time and place'.

'He died with great constancy without show of fear: which seemed very well in so venerable a person, and by reason of his age his death hath made great impression in many'.

'Three or four times they offered him his life if he would take the oath; but he always refused, saying he would willingly swear all love and lawful obedience to his King, for whom he prayed all his lifetime, but rather than take this oath he would die a thousand times'.

Father John Knaresborough (*Sufferings of the Catholics*, c.1720) gives further information from the *Exemplar Literarum* of 1616, 'The venerable old man was securely tied on the hurdle and dragged through the streets of York to the gallows. The crowd of spectators was unusually great, not that the putting of a priest to death was a sight so very strange . . . but the great age of Mr Atkinson and the general esteem he had gained by his exemplary life and conversation, even among the Protestants of those parts, excited a curiosity in thousands to be present at the place of execution to see the comportment of this ancient and godly priest in this last stage of his life'.

'Thus after a little time spent in private devotions, and some few words to the Catholics to encourage them to constancy in their sufferings and perseverance in the profession of the Catholic Faith, he delivered himself to the executioner and was turned off'.

In prison no allowance had been made for his old age and so it was in his execution. He was shown no mercy and suffered the full rigour of the law in all its cruelty. He was hanged, drawn and quartered at the Knavesmire on 11 March, 1616.

Nicholas Postgate

Each summer every year, in that part of the wild North Yorkshire Moors known so aptly as Blackamoor, Catholics gather in their thousands from far and near to celebrate Mass and honour the memory of Father Nicholas Postgate, the Priest of the Moors and the best known and most loved of all the Yorkshire Martyrs.

In the little moorland parishes of Egton Bridge and Ugthorpe, the local Catholics hold him dear as one of their own and speak of him today with an easy familiarity, as though he were some well-loved Parish Priest recently removed from their midst. To them, he is always Father Postgate with the emphasis on the 'Father', and with typical Yorkshire bluntness they express their loyal impatience that the formal process of canonisation is so slow when everyone knows, they say, that Father Postgate is already a saint in Heaven.

Father Postgate still seems to live on the Moors and the people for whom he gave his life have never forgotten the greatness of his person, the warmth of his character and the holiness of his life. For three hundred years a great oral tradition has been passed on from generation to generation and the story-tellers of these rural communities have ensured that Father Postgate is as well-known today as ever he was in the past.

Such oral tradition, of course, powerful as it is, demands the support of external historical evidence lest minor inaccuracies and occasional lapses into wishful thinking should diminish the value of what these people say. Perhaps there has been a too easy acceptance of all the details; perhaps at times strangers are led to believe what they want to believe. Certainly, it would seem the time has now come for a more critical examination of all the available information so that with the help of modern scholarship, Father Postgate is fitted more securely into the context of his own times and the context of today.

Sometimes, of course, the oral tradition is too powerful for even the historians to contradict. The people are quite unanimous that Nicholas Postgate was born at Kirkdale House in Egton Bridge. The eminent historian, J.C.H. Aveling (*Northern Catholics*, p. 348) maintains he was the son of a prosperous farmer, James Postgate of Deane Hall, Egton, but few accept this suggestion. Father Godfrey Anstruther OP (*Seminary Priests*, vol. 2, p. 249) names Ugglebarnby as the Martyr's birthplace, but again little acceptance is forthcoming. Kirkdale House it is from constant tradition, and the tradition is fully supported by Father John Knaresborough who was seven years old when Nicholas Postgate was martyred but who spoke regularly from about 1708 onwards with the Egton people who knew the priest personally. About 1720 Father Knaresborough put it all in writing. (Humberside County Record Office, Beverley, DDEV/67/2).

Nicholas Postgate was born in no great mansion. 'Despite its high sounding name', wrote Father John Mulholland in 1975 (*In the Steps of Father Postgate*, p. 8), 'it was a cottage near the bridge over the Esk at Egton Bridge. It must have been a poor cottage. People in Egton can still remember the ruins of the cottage with its walls two or three feet high'.

Oral tradition establishes the place of birth for Nicholas Postgate but is indefinite about his date of birth. Historians can do little better. The Parish Registers of Egton go back only to 1622 and even if there were Parish Records it does not necessarily follow that a Catholic birth or baptism would appear in them.

The Third Douai Diary states that Nicholas Postgate was twenty-one when he was admitted to the College in 1621. This would mean he was born in 1599 or 1600. Bishop Richard Challoner (*Memoirs of Missionary Priests*, 1924 edition, p. 547) says merely that Nicholas Postgate was born 'about the end of the sixteenth century'. From other sources there are other slight variations. Father Postgate himself is reported as stating at the time of his arrest in 1679 that he was 'about the age of four score years', (Public Record Office, Assizes, 45/12/2, no. 71) This would mean he was born in 1598. According to a broadsheet published on 7 August 1679, he was then 'about 90' and therefore born in 1588. Father John Warner SJ says he was more than eighty in 1679; the inscription on Father Postgate's coffin proclaimed his age as eighty-two. The very reliable Father John Knaresborough (1708, DDEV/67/3, p. 275) says he was 'full four score years and three', and Mr Thomas Ward (*England's Reformation*, 1710, p. 102) agrees poetically 'eighty years and three times one'. Perhaps the best that can be said from all this evidence is that Nicholas Postgate was born sometime between 1588 and 1600, and that 1599 is the most likely date.

There is no doubt however that Nicholas Postgate came from a most dedicated Catholic family. 'His parents were Catholics and great sufferers for their religion', wrote Bishop Challoner. His father James died in 1602, but his mother, formerly Margaret Watson, lived on until 1624, to ensure the religious education of Nicholas and his brothers Matthew and William.

They lived in difficult days for faithful Catholics but the religious influence of the home was augmented by the strength of the Egton Catholic community. The Postgates were not the only Catholics in the Egton of those days, as Peacock's list of Yorkshire Catholics in 1604 shows with such surprising clarity: 'Christopher Consett and Ellis Knaggs; Christopher Simpson and Dorothy Pearson; Henry Lawson and Dorothy Marshal; George Knaggs and Ellis Dawson; Christopher Taylor and Jane Burton; all these lived together as man and wife and suspected to be secretly married; Edward Simpson, Henry Lawson, George Knaggs, Christopher Consett, Jane (sic) Postgate, widow,: John Roe and Ralph Harwood had children baptised privately'. (Peacock, p. 95). Peacock was investigating on behalf of the Government and it is very unlikely that his list should be complete. There were many more Catholics in Egton than he noticed but even the numbers he has produced are remarkable for a small village, and the number of secret marriages and secret baptisms point firmly to the regular presence of a priest or priests.

Within this community of the Faith, Nicholas Postgate grew up. It was a community isolated from the rest of the country but it was certainly not a community isolated from the activities of the Catholic Church. Blackamoor had long been an area where secret Catholics flourished. As early as 1561 the deprived Marian

Bishop of Hull, Robert Pursglove, had been confined under bond to a twelve mile radius of his residence at Ugthorpe, and if J.C.H. Aveling is right about his orthodoxy he must have had a powerful effect on the Catholic life of the district. 'He remains a fascinating case of which we should like to know much more'. (*Northern Catholics*, p. 40)

The Catholic Radcliffes of Mulgrave Castle bought the manor of Ugthorpe in 1565, and from 1587 Mrs Katherine Radcliffe used it as her home and as a safe centre for the many fugitive priests arriving in secret on the north east coast. There were harbourers of priests too at the Cholmley house at Whitby where Lady Katherine Scrope presided over her ecclesiastical charges. At Dunsley, also, Christopher Stonehouse was always prepared to welcome priests.

Much closer to Egton was the missionary headquarters for Yorkshire and Durham established by Father John Mush at Grosmont about the year 1580. Here the Hodgson family, tenants of the Cholmleys, organised a safe house for the reception of priests from overseas and a place of rest and withdrawal for the harassed priests on the mission. In 1592, the apostate Thomas Clarke could give the names of twenty-one priests to the Government and insist that he had seen each one of them at Grosmont. He could also acknowledge in the same report that he himself had said Mass in 'Glaisdale, one Postgate's at Egton, Mulgrave, Ugthorpe, Fylingdales and Whitby'. (G.W. Boddy, *Northern Catholic History*, vol. 19, art. 1). On 29 May 1599, this same Clarke wrote to Cecil, 'Blackamoor is a bishopric of papists and Grosmont Abbey the head house, wherein Crawfurth the bishop lies. . . All traitors that come from beyond the seas to that coast are received there, and by means of that house, three parts of the people in Blackamoor are become papist'. (Boddy, op. cit.)

A week later, violence broke out between the Catholics and the Government agents, and on 26 June Lord Sheffield took reprisals on the Catholics with an armed assault on their stronghold of Grosmont, only to find that the Catholic intelligence services were ahead of him and the place was abandoned and empty. For a short while prudence dictated that the Catholics should lie low, but John Hodgson, his wife Jane and their son Richard were soon back in residence to continue their work for priests.

The story-tellers of Egton would do full justice to these heroic exploits in their frequently repeated stories and the young Nicholas Postgate must have been inspired by the achievements of his ancestors even as the young people of today are inspired by the achievements of Nicholas Postgate himself. With such inspiration in such circumstances, it is not surprising that Nicholas should consider his own vocation to the priesthood, but for some reason he delayed his departure for the English College at Douai.

As he advanced through his teens, the forces of the Crown became more oppressive on the Moors and Catholic activity consequently more subdued. Open opposition gave way to a more subtle but no less determined approach. Catholics expressed themselves by forming groups of actors who innocently toured the surrounding villages with a quite innocuous repertoire of plays and songs and then used the intervals or interludes in their entertainment to proclaim their Faith and attack the Established Church. A group of such actors was arrested in January 1616 and charged at Helmsley Quarter Sessions with being 'common players of interludes, vagabonds and sturdy beggars'. Five of the eight accused were from Egton and one of them was Nicholas Postgate, described as a labourer, thirteen years of age. The age of the boy causes some difficulty because the future martyr would be over sixteen at the time, but J.C.H. Aveling has no doubt in asserting his acceptance of a positive identification (*Northern Catholics*, p. 290).

At last, in 1621, Nicholas Postgate crossed the seas to Douai to begin his studies for the priesthood. His previous education had been sufficient for him to undertake the ordinary course of studies, and he was entered on the rolls as an alumnus or free scholar; but being already a man, an offering for expenses was expected, and the sum of three hundred florins was handed over.

The Douai Diary charts the progress of Nicholas Postgate through the English College. Having assumed the name of Whitmore, he took the customary Missionary Oath on 12 March 1623, and was ordained priest by Archbishop Paul Baudot at Arras on 20 March 1628. He did not return at once to England but remained in Douai as College Sacristan, and the Diary praises him for performing this task 'with great fidelity, diligence, and in a manner of great benefit to the College'.

Father Postgate left Douai on 29 June 1630 to begin his long apostolate of almost fifty years on the English Mission. Of course it is difficult to trace his movements, and at times he seems to have disappeared completely. Historians have to rely on the account he gave himself at the very end of his life, when charged with the crime of his priesthood. He spoke under pressure, possibly dazed from the treatment he had received from his captors, and certainly on guard lest he should give away so much information as to imperil the lives of others.

The official account of this examination at Brompton on 9 December 1678 states, 'He says that about forty years since he lived at Saxton with the Lady Hungate until she died, and since he has lived with the old Lady Dunbar, but how late it is since he knows not, and he says that of late he has had no certain residence but had travelled about among his friends'. (Public Record Office, Assizes, 45/12/2 no. 71). It is from this evidence mainly that the outline record of Father Postgate's missionary career is put together. His vague reference to 'about forty years since he lived at Saxton' could only refer to his first appointment which was in fact forty-eight years before. From 1630 he lived at Saxton near Tadcaster in the West Riding and worked as chaplain to Lady Hungate. His appointment would end with her death in 1642 and this fixes the date when he became chaplain to 'old Lady Dunbar'. At first she lived with her husband, the first Viscount Dunbar, possibly at Burton Constable Hall, but on his death in 1645 she moved to nearby Halsham some twelve miles to the south in Holderness. Lady Dunbar died in 1659 and Father Postgate's appointment would be terminated.

It is unusual that a simple moorland priest like Father Postgate should be chaplain to a family as important as the Constables. They were the hereditary Lords Paramount of the Seigneurie of Holderness and among the most powerful Catholic families of the land. Father David Quinlan traces an Egton connection and suggests in the 1967 edition of his book *The Father Postgate Story*, (p. 7) that Sir Henry Constable, first Viscount Dunbar, was the son of Thomas Smith of Bridgeholme Green, Egton. He corrects himself in the 1973 edition to assert that it was Lady Dunbar who was daughter to the same Thomas Smith. This all seems highly improbable since in those days families of such different ranks did not inter-marry. Joseph Stanislaus Hansom gives the true pedigree of the Dunbars (Catholic Record Society, vol. XIV, p. 322) and shows that Viscount Dunbar was a true Constable by blood and that he married Mary, daughter of Sir John Tufton of Hothfield, Kent. Father Postgate's appointment then did not depend on any local or family connection but can be seen only as a reward for meritorious service to Lady Hungate and as a sign of the high esteem he had earned among the recusant families.

From the death of Lady Dunbar in 1659 until his reappearance on the Moors in the early 1660s, it is very difficult to trace Father Postgate's movements. There is a strong tradition that he spent some of this time at Everingham in East Yorkshire. He was certainly well known to the Constables of Everingham. He was present as an honoured guest at the family dinner on Christmas Day, 1662 (Catholic Record Society, vol. XXVII, pp. 261–273); in 1665, Sir Philip Constable of Everingham left him £5 in his will, (Catholic Record Society, vol. IV, p. 269); George Constable of Everingham left him £1 in his will in 1672, (Catholic Record Society, vol. XXVII, p. 266). All this however is evidence of a close friendship with the Constables rather than any proof of residence, and of course all branches of the Constable family would know the priest from their visits to Lady Dunbar at Halsham. If the evidence for Father Postgate's chaplaincy at Everingham is uncertain, the tradition is not, and the Documents of the Cause accept rather cautiously 'that he seems to have lived for some time with a junior branch of the Constable family at Everingham'.

It is also maintained by Father David Quinlan, (*The Father Postgate Story*, 1973 edition, p. 3) that 'at times, he (Father Postgate) resided with the Saltmarsh family at Kilvington Hall, near Thirsk, and the Meynell family at Kilvington Castle'. The tradition in support of these residences is not as strong as the tradition for the earlier residence at Everingham and no factual evidence seems to be available. The statement by Father Peter Saltmarsh SJ (Foley, Records SJ, vol. VI, p. 454) that he was baptised by Father Postgate at Kilvington in 1658 cannot imply that the priest was resident because at that time he was still chaplain to Lady Dunbar in Holderness.

What is certain is that between 1659 and about 1663 Father Postgate was experiencing difficulty in finding a permanent place of residence. It was a time when the Catholic gentry of England were becoming less numerous, or at best were in rather reduced circumstances and unable to afford a chaplain. Hence there were fewer resident chaplains and more travelling priests who served larger districts and found shelter where they could. Such conditions forced many priests to look beyond the sheltered confines of the country mansion to the increasing needs of the poorer Catholics further afield. Father Postgate was perhaps yearning for the company of the poor and especially of his own folk on the moors of North Yorkshire. He was sixty years of age at least; he had spent over thirty years on the Yorkshire mission; now in his old age he moved back to Blackamoor.

At about the time of this return he wrote a most important letter about his missionary activities to Dr George Leyburn, President of the English College at Douai, and the President was so impressed that he sent a copy of this letter to Cardinal Francesco Barberini, Protector of England, as an example of the extraordinary work and achievement of the Douai priests on the English Mission. From internal evidence this letter is firmly dated for 1664, and therefore contrary to popular belief cannot refer to Father Postgate's work on the Moors. It refers rather to his thirty-four years as a priest in other parts of Yorkshire. Only when he mentions that 'at this moment I have quite six hundred penitents and could have more if I wished' is there the possibility that he might be alluding to the people of Blackamoor.

Father Postgate writes, (Vatican Archives, Barb. Lat. 2184, f129) 'I have always worked to help poor Catholics . . . I live as a poor man amongst the poor . . . I often repeat to myself those words, "Why look for rest when you were put into the world to labour?" . . . what I lack is not the will but help; I am working right to the limits of my strength . . .' In this letter, Father Postgate gives his own personal statistics for his thirty-four years of ministry: five hundred and ninety-three Baptisms, two hundred and twenty-six Marriages, seven hundred and nineteen Burials, and he adds that with converts, he has increased the Church by two thousand four hundred souls.

In his commentary on this letter, Father David Quinlan goes

right to the heart of the matter: 'of his manner of life Father Postgate used a luminous description. He said that he had lived among "the poorer sort of people", to whose circumstances he conformed as to dress, diet and lodgings. He did this "just short of pride". That is the only autobiographical account we have of him. It is marked by great simplicity of soul, insight and a delicate sense of humour. "I embraced poverty just short of pride" tells us more of the hidden priest than anything else we know of him, both in the fact and in his expression of it'. (*The Father Postgate Story*, 1967, p. 10).

Father Postgate spent the rest of his life on the Moors. He himself claimed that he 'had no certain residence but travelled about among his friends', but this statement was made under some duress during his examination by Government agents at Brompton. Perhaps he was trying to withhold information. The local tradition is quite clear that he made his home in a small thatched cottage near Ugthorpe. A more recent building stands on the site today and is still known as the Hermitage, although very little remains of the original.

Father Postgate's house was described in an article signed simply JW in the *Catholic Magazine* for 1838. 'I have visited that cell, for it still stands where it stood. It is one of the poorest huts of the poor, a mere cattle-shed in appearance, its little chimney alone denoting it to be a human habitation. Looking towards the north, the west and the south a black moor presents its desolate aspect; but on the east a long tract of cultivated land stretches like a promontory before whose brow a small sea-bay is visible. I stopped to enter the lowly hut, where pride must be put off with the hat. It consists of two small apartments, one emphatically styled 'the house' in which domestic duties are done; the other a place of rest; both are on the ground floor, which is paved with uneven stones. The thatched roof is just overhead; the lattice windows are very narrow and deeply indented in the clumsy walls; there is a hearth for a peat fire'.

The authenticity of Father Postgate's cottage does not rest only on the oral tradition of his people. Thomas Ward, who was born at Danby Castle in 1652 and became a Catholic about the year 1672, knew Father Postgate personally. He refers to the priest in his book *England's Reformation*, published in 1710, and in the fourth canto writes:

A thatched cottage was the cell
Where this contemplative did dwell;
Two miles from Mulgrave Castle it stood,
Sheltered by snow-drifts, not by wood;
Tho' there he lived to that great age,
It was a dismal hermitage,
But God plac'd there the saint's abode,
For Blackamor's greater good.

From this tiny headquarters Father Postgate roamed the moors from Guisborough to Pickering. His journeyings were extensive and the moorland tracks must have been difficult especially for a man of his age, yet he is always depicted as travelling on foot. A very old picture by an unknown artist in Whitby Museum shows him as an old man with a long white beard, but significantly clutching the stout staff of a walker in his left hand.

It is commonly asserted that Father Postgate escaped capture because he lived so secretly on the isolated moors, and there are stories of his assumed name, his disguise as a gardener, his favourite hiding places and his skill in evading capture. This may not be altogether a true picture. Father Postgate's success was not that nobody knew who he was. The last place for anyone to seek to conceal his identity is among the scattered villages of an open countryside, where every stranger is subject to scrutiny and then figures prominently in local conversations. Father Postgate's success, it would seem was that everybody knew who he was but loved and revered him so much that as long as he maintained a low profile nobody was prepared to betray him to the authorities. When he was eventually betrayed, the deed was perpetrated by a complete outsider who stirred the local people into action, and then indeed the witnesses confessed that for a long time they had known him to be a priest.

William Cockerill, the constable, said 'he had often seen the person now apprehended by the name of Postgate as he passed along the country and that he was generally reputed and spoken to be a popish priest'. Another constable, Robert Langdale, said, 'he had often heard of the prisoner Postgate and that for many years he had generally been accounted a popish priest'. Elizabeth

Baxter said that 'she had several times seen Nicholas Postgate, the reputed popish priest'. Elizabeth Wood said that 'she had known the aforesaid Nicholas Postgate, ten or twelve years and had heard him say Mass'. Richard Morris said that 'he knew one Mr Postgate, a popish priest' (Public Record Office, Assizes, 45/12/2 no.71). Such evidence from Government servants and lapsed Catholics suggests that Father Postgate was well known as a 'popish priest' and that his presence was tolerated by those who did not share his religion, because they recognised his virtue. Perhaps Father Postgate might have lived on to die a peaceful death on his beloved moors if only John Reeves had stayed in London.

On 3 October 1678, a resolution of the House of Commons spoke of a 'damnable and hellish plot, contrived and carried on by the popish recusants for the assassinating and murdering of the King, and for subverting the Government and rooting out and destroying the Protestant religion', and next day at a conference, the House of Lords 'readily and unanimously agreed'. (Journals of the House of Commons, IX, p. 530). Of course there was no such Catholic plot. The Catholics were enjoying a period of peace and quiet throughout the country and had no wish to stir up the old animosities and violence. The Plot was an invention of the imagination of Titus Oates, a most unsavoury character, but despite his evil reputation his words were believed, and a wave of bitter persecution of the Catholics once more swept through England.

John Reeves, a servant of Sir Edmundbury Godfrey in London, was much affected by the anti-Catholic agitation occasioned by the alleged Plot and further incensed when his employer was murdered and the Catholics blamed for the crime. Full of bitterness, he came to Whitby determined to avenge himself on whatever Catholics he could find. The opportunity for action presented itself when he heard a report that Matthew Lyth of Redbarns, near Littlebeck below Ugglebarnby Moor, had said at a wedding 'You talk of papists and Protestants, but when the roast is ready, I know who shall have first cut'. Supposing this to be a threat that the Catholics were contemplating an uprising, Reeves took a small raiding party to Redbarns, expecting that he might find some arms or ammunition. Instead he found Father

Postgate (Father David Quinlan, *The Father Postgate Story*, 1973, pp. 9–16).

The details of Father Postgate's arrest are contained in the records preserved of his judicial examination. (Public Record Office, Assizes, 45/12/2, no. 71). These give the place as stated and show that the priest was caught in possession of Catholic books, wafers and other incriminating evidence. When asked about his priesthood, Father Postgate replied, 'Let them prove it'. And it is Henry Cockerill who testifies 'that the said Matthew Lyth did endeavour to hide and conceal the said Postgate, standing before him until the said John Reeves did pull him away'.

The captured priest was taken about twenty miles south to Brompton to make his appearance before Sir William Cayley, a Justice of the Peace. No information is available as to why he was taken so far and to this particular Justice of the Peace. There were many Justices more conveniently situated near Ugglebarnby but perhaps local feeling was too strong to allow such a well-beloved person to be tried in the midst of his own people.

Father Postgate was first examined at Brompton on 9 December 1678, and would seem to have remained in captivity there until his further examinations on 6 and 7 March 1679. He was then sent to York and his trial took place at the Lent Assizes. Official records of this trial have been lost and the exact date is unknown but it must have been some time between the 7th and the 26th March, 1679. The latest date for the trial is fixed by the date of a letter of Mr John Ryther (related by marriage to the Radcliffes of Ugthorpe) in which he states, 'Old Mr Postgate is found guilty of being a priest'. (Father John Knaresborough's Collections, 1679, Humberside Record Office, DDEV/67/2). It is clear from all sources that Father Postgate was not charged with any involvement in the supposed Plot but was charged simply for being a priest. Once more the Statute of 1585 'against Jesuits, seminary priests and such other like disobedient persons' was invoked.

A lyrical writer in the Gentleman's Magazine has achieved some fame by his description of the judge as a scarlet-coated huntsman crying the hounds on to their quarry, but in fact the judge was scrupulously fair and showed the priest as much kindness as he could while still administering the law. In another part of his letter of 26 March 1679 John Ryther writes, 'Everyone speaks the Judge to be civil, though some well effected Justice of the Peace complains of the gaoler for having allowed the gentlemen the liberty of the town'. (Father Knaresborough's Collections, 1679, Humberside Record Office DDEV/67/2). Indeed despite the raging fury of those who believed in the reality of the Popish Plot there was an underlying diffidence among responsible people and a reluctance to return to the barbarism of previous years. The Law had to be observed and Father Postgate was undoubtedly a priest and therefore technically a traitor. As such he was condemned to death, but the authorities were not altogether agreed that the execution should be carried out. Accordingly for the next four months Father Postgate was kept a prisoner in York Castle, while the authorities considered what they should do about 'the divers popish priests who have been condemned in several counties'. Father Postgate spent his time in prayerful preparation for death and in receiving numerous visitors with what Father John Warner (1685) called 'the most open arms of charity'.

At last, on 11 July 1679, the Privy Council issued its instructions: 'It was this day ordered by their Lordships in Council that the respective Judges who go the circuits where the said priests remain, do forthwith give direction that they be executed according to Law' (Public Record Office, PC, 2/63, p. 173). In accordance with this instruction, Father Postgate was told that he was to die on 7 August. On the morning of that day two women, Mrs Charles Fairfax of York and Mrs Meynell of Kilvington, visited the priest to receive sacramental absolution in his cell. Later Mrs Fairfax reported personally to Father John Knaresborough the details of this visit and how Father Postgate 'seeing them in great concern, came up to them with a cheerful countenance'. (Letter of 15 October 1705, DDEV/67/2 in Humberside Record Office).

Father John Warner SJ (*History of the Oates Plot*, 1685) confirms that the old recusant custom of preparing a martyr for his death was fully carried out. Father Postgate was presented with new white clothes 'so that he might enter as if to the nuptials of the Lamb in his wedding'. The old priest was then placed on the hurdle and dragged through the streets of York to the Knavesmire, but Father Warner maintains that this journey resembled the triumphant progress of a conqueror rather than the passage of a condemned man to his death.

The substance of the last speech of Father Postgate from the gallows has been preserved in a contemporary broadsheet of 7 August 1679. He said, 'I die in the Catholic religion, out of which there is no salvation. Mr Sheriff, you know I die not for the Plot, but for my religion. I pray God bless the King and the Royal Family. Mr Sheriff, I pray you tell the King that I never offended him in any manner of way. I pray God give him his grace and the light of truth. I forgive all that have wronged me and brought me to this death, and I desire forgiveness of all people'. Father Nicholas Postgate was then hanged, drawn and quartered. His final prayer was answered: his King, Charles II, was given 'the light of truth' on his deathbed six years later and died a Catholic.

As for Father Postgate, his mortal remains were carried away on a four wheeled cart for burial by his friends, and even some non-Catholics followed it in procession. (Father Warner's statement, 1685). His place of burial is not now known, but Father John Knaresborough (Humberside record office, DDEV/67/3 p. 275) relates that a copper plate was thrown into the coffin and that this plate bore the following inscription: 'Here lyeth that Reverend and pious divine, Dr Nicholas Postgate, who was educated in the English College at Doway. And after he had laboured fifty years (to the admirable benefit and conversion of hundred (sic) of souls) was at last advanced to a glorious crown of martyrdom at the city of York on the seventh of August 1679, having been a priest 51 years, aged 82'.

Appendix

A list of those martyrs who have been formally recognised by the Church and who have connections with the Middlesbrough Diocese.

Abbreviations

b	born	L	layperson
c	captured	NR	North Riding
ER	East Riding	SP	Seminary Priest
H	hanged	WR	West Riding
HDQ	hanged, drawn, quartered.		

SAINT JOHN FISHER	b Beverley; Cardinal Bishop of Rochester	Beheaded, London 22 June, 1535
SAINT LUKE KIRBY	b Bedale; NR; SP	HDQ London, 30 May, 1582
SAINT MARGARET CLITHEROW	b York; L	York 25 March, 1586
SAINT JOHN BOSTE	SP; worked in NR	HDQ Durham, 24 July, 1594
SAINT HENRY WALPOLE	b Norfolk, Jesuit; c Kilham, ER	HDQ York, 7 April, 1595
BLESSED JOHN ROCHESTER	b Essex; Carthusian priest.	H in chains, York, 11 May, 1537
BLESSED JAMES WALWORTH	Carthusian priest.	H in chains, York, 11 May, 1537

BLESSED THOMAS PERCY	Earl of Northumberland; of Wressle Castle, ER.	Beheaded, York, 22 August, 1572
BLESSED JOHN NELSON	b Skelton near York; SP	HDQ London, 3 February, 1578
BLESSED WILLIAM LACEY	b Horton, WR; SP	HDQ York, 22 August, 1582
BLESSED RICHARD KIRKMAN	b Skipton, WR; SP	HDQ York, 22 August, 1582
BLESSED JAMES THOMPSON	b York; SP.	HDQ York, 28 November, 1582
BLESSED WILLIAM HART	b Somerset; SP	HDQ York, 15 March, 1583
BLESSED RICHARD THIRKELD	b Coniscliffe-on-Tees SP.	HDQ York, 29 May, 1583
BLESSED RICHARD LANGLEY	of Ousethorpe, near Pocklington; L ER	H York, 1 December, 1586
BLESSED JOHN HEWETT	b York; SP	H London 5 October, 1588
BLESSED JOHN AMIAS (ANNE)	b Wakefield, WR; SP.	HDQ York, 15 March, 1589
BLESSED ROBERT DALBY	b Hemingbrough ER; SP	HDQ York, 15 March, 1589
BLESSED ANTHONY MIDDLETON	b Middleton Tyas NR; SP	HDQ London, 6 May, 1590
BLESSED WILLIAM HARRINGTON	b Felixkirk, NR; SP	HDQ London, 18 February, 1594

BLESSED ALEXANDER RAWLINS	b Oxfordshire; SP	HDQ York, 7 April, 1595
BLESSED WILLIAM FREEMAN	b Menthorpe, ER; SP	HDQ Warwick, 13 August, 1595
BLESSED HENRY ABBOT	of Howden, ER; L.	HDQ York, 4 July, 1597
BLESSED WILLIAM ANDLEBY	b Etton, ER; SP	HDQ York, 4 July, 1597
BLESSED THOMAS WARCOP	of Gatenby, NR; L	H York, 4 July, 1597
BLESSED EDWARD FULTHROP	b Yorkshire; L	HDQ York, 4 July, 1597
BLESSED JOHN PIBUSH	b Thirsk, NR; SP	HDQ London, 18 February, 1601
BLESSED ROBERT WATKINSON	b Hemingbrough ER; SP	HDQ London, 20 April, 1602
BLESSED THOMAS WELBOURNE	b Hutton Bushel, NR; L.	HDQ York, 1 August, 1605
BLESSED EDWARD OLDCORNE	b York; Jesuit	HDQ Worcester, 7 April, 1607
BLESSED THOMAS TUNSTAL	of Wycliffe, NR; Benedictine	HDQ Norwich, 13 July, 1616
BLESSED JOHN LOCKWOOD	b Sowerby, NR; SP	HDQ York, 13 April, 1642

BLESSED EDWARD CATHERICK	b Carlton, Richmondshire; SP	HDQ York, 13 April, 1642
BLESSED THOMAS THWING	b Heworth, York; SP	HDQ York, 23 October, 1680

The Venerable martyrs to be beatified in 1987

VENERABLE HUGH TAYLOR	SP.	HDQ York, 26 November, 1585
VENERABLE MARMADUKE BOWES	of Angram Grange, NR; L	H York, 27 November, 1585
VENERABLE FRANCIS INGLEBY	b Ripley, WR; SP.	HDQ York, 3 June, 1586
VENERABLE JOHN FINGLEY	b Barmby, ER; SP	HDQ York, 8 August, 1586
VENERABLE ROBERT BICKERDIKE	b Knaresborough, WR; L	HDQ York, about August, 1586
VENERABLE ALEXANDER CROWE	b Howden, ER; SP	HDQ York, 30 November, 1586
VENERABLE EDMUND SYKES	b Leeds, WR; SP.	HDQ York, 23 March, 1587
VENERABLE GEORGE DOUGLAS	b Edinburgh; SP.	HDQ York, 9 September, 1587
VENERABLE RICHARD SIMPSON	b Well, Bedale, NR; SP	HDQ Derby, 24 July, 1588

VENERABLE EDWARD BURDEN	b Cleveland; SP.	HDQ York, about 29 November, 1588
VENERABLE WILLIAM SPENSER	b Gisburn, WR; SP.	HDQ York, 24 September, 1589
VENERABLE ROBERT HARDESTY	b Yorkshire; L	H York, 24 September, 1589
VENERABLE JOHN HOGG	b Cleveland; SP (Ugthorpe?)	HDQ Durham, 27 May, 1590
VENERABLE ROBERT THORPE	b Yorkshire; SP (Holderness?)	HDQ York, 31 May, 1591
VENERABLE THOMAS WATKINSON	b Menthorpe, ER; L	H York, 31 May, 1591
VENERABLE JOSEPH LAMBTON	b Malton, NR; SP	HDQ Newcastle on Tyne about 31 July, 1592
VENERABLE ANTHONY PAGE	b Harrow, Middlesex c York; SP	HDQ York, 20 April, 1593
VENERABLE EDWARD OSBALDESTON	b Osbaldeston, Lancashire; c Tollerton, NR; SP.	HDQ York, 16 November, 1594
VENERABLE GEORGE ERRINGTON	b Hirst, Northumberland; L	HDQ York, 29 November, 1596
VENERABLE WILLIAM KNIGHT	b South Duffield, ER: L	HDQ York, 29 November, 1596

VENERABLE WILLIAM GIBSON	b near Ripon; L. c Brafferton, NR.	HDQ York, 29 November, 1596
VENERABLE JOHN BRETTON	b near Wakefield, WR; L	H York, 1 April, 1598
VENERABLE PETER SNOW	b Richmondshire; SP	HDQ York, 15 June, 1598
VENERABLE RALPH GIMSTOW	b Knaresborough, WR; L	H York, 15 June, 1598
VENERABLE CHRISTOPHER WHARTON	b Middleton, WR; SP	HDQ York, 28 March, 1600
VENERABLE EDWARD THWING	b Heworth, York; SP	HDQ Lancaster 26 July, 1600
VENERABLE THOMAS PALASER	b Ellerton, Richmondshire; SP	HDQ Durham, 8 September, 1600
VENERABLE JOHN NORTON	Wath, NR; L	H Durham, 8 September, 1600
VENERABLE JOHN TALBOT	b Thornton-le-Street, NR; L	H Durham, 8 September, 1600
VENERABLE ROBERT MIDDLETON	b York; SP/Jesuit	HDQ Lancaster, 3 April, 1601
VENERABLE MATTHEW FLATHERS	b Otley, WR; SP	HDQ York, 21 March, 1608
VENERABLE THOMAS ATKINSON	b Yorkshire; SP; c Willitoft, ER;	HDQ York, 11 March, 1616
VENERABLE NICHOLAS POSTGATE	b Egton Bridge, NR: SP.	HDQ York, 7 August, 1679.

The causes of the following Venerable Martyrs were postponed for further research in 1929

VENERABLE RICHARD HORNER	b Bolton Bridge, Yorks; SP	HDQ York, 4 September, 1598
VENERABLE JAMES HARRISON	b Yorkshire; SP	HDQ York, 22 March, 1602
VENERABLE ANTHONY BATES (or Battie)	b Yorkshire; L	H York, 22 March, 1602
VENERABLE BRIAN CANSFIELD	Jesuit	Died in prison, York, 1645

The causes of the following martyrs were introduced in 1874, but then postponed in order to seek further evidence. Since their causes have not been formally accepted, they do not have the title 'Venerable'.

THOMAS METHAM	b Howden, ER; Jesuit	Died in prison, Wisbech, June, 1592
MATTHEW HARRISON	b Yorkshire; SP	HDQ York, 1599
MRS ELEANOR HUNT	Ripley; WR; L	Died in prison, York, 1600
EDWARD WILKES	b Knaresborough, WR; c Malton, NR; SP	Died in prison, York, about May, 1642
WILLIAM ALLISON	SP	Died in prison, York, 1681
BENEDICT CONSTABLE	b Yorkshire; Benedictine	Died in prison, Durham, 1683.

Bibliography

OFFICIAL PRESENTATION OF DOCUMENTS on the martyrdom of Venerable George Haydock and Companions, published by the sacred Congregation for the Causes of Saints, Rome, 1981 (Documents of the Cause).

ANSTRUTHER, G, OP — The Seminary Priests, 1968.

AVELING, J.C.H. — Post-Reformation Catholicism in East Yorkshire, 1960
The Catholic Recusants of the West Riding, 1963
The Northern Catholics, 1966
Catholic Recusancy in York, 1970
The Handle and the Axe, 1976

BOSSY, J. — The English Catholic Community, 1975

BRIDGETT, T.E. C.ss.R. — Queen Elizabeth and the Catholic Hierarchy Deposed, 1889

BURTON, E.H. and POLLEN, J.H. (SJ) — Lives of the English Martyrs, 1914

CAMM, B., OSB — Forgotten Shrines, 1910

CHALLONER, R. — Memoirs of the Missionary Priests, 1741

CLARIDGE, M. — Margaret Clitherow, 1966

FOLEY, H, SJ — Records of the English Province of the Society of Jesus, 1877–1883.

GILLOW, J. — A Literary and Biographical History of the English Catholics, 1885–1902.

HAMILTON, E. — The Priest of the Moors, 1980.

HIRST, J.H. — The Blockhouses of Hull, 1913.

HOLMES, P. — Resistance and Compromise: Political Thought of Elizabethan Catholics, 1982.

HUGHES, P. — The Reformation in England, 1963

LEYS, M.D.R. — Catholics in England, 1961

LUNN, D., OSB — English Benedictines, (1540–1688), 1980.

MAGEE, B. — The English Recusants, 1938

MATHEW, D. — Catholicism in England, 1955

MEYER, A.O. — England and the Catholic Church under Queen Elizabeth, 1916–1967.

MOREY, A., OSB — Catholic Subjects of Elizabeth I, 1978

MORRIS, J., SJ — Troubles of our Catholic Forefathers, 1872

MULHOLLAND, J. — In the Steps of Father Postgate, 1975.

MYERSCOUGH, J.A., SJ — The Martyrs of Durham, 1955.

NORMAN, E. — Roman Catholicism in England, 1985.

PEACOCK. — List of Roman Catholics in the County of York, 1604, pub. 1872.

POLLEN, J.H., SJ — Acts of the English Martyrs, 1891.

PUBLICATIONS OF THE CATHOLIC RECORD SOCIETY, 1904–1985.

QUINLAN, D. — The Father Postgate Story, 1967 and 1973.

RAINE, J. (Editor) — History and Antiquities of the Parish of Hemingbrough by Thomas Burton, 1888.

ROWSE, A.L. — The Expansion of Elizabethan England, 1955.

TIERNEY, M.A. — Dodd's Church History of England, 1840.

TRIMBLE, W.R. — The Catholic Laity in Elizabethan England, 1964.

VICTORIA COUNTY HISTORIES.

WATKIN, E.I. — Roman Catholicism in England, 1957.

PERIODICALS

AMPLEFORTH JOURNAL

BIOGRAPHICAL STUDIES

NORTHERN CATHOLIC HISTORY

RECUSANT HISTORY

USHAW MAGAZINE

Index